Totemism

Totemism

By CLAUDE LÉVI-STRAUSS, PROFESSOR
OF SOCIAL ANTHROPOLOGY, COLLÈGE DE FRANCE, PARIS

Translated from the French by RODNEY NEEDHAM,
Lecturer in Social Anthropology, University of Oxford

BEACON PRESS   BOSTON

First published in France in 1962 by Presses
Universitaires de France, under the title,
Le totémisme aujourd'hui
Copyright © 1962 by Presses Universitaires de France
First English translation published in this
Beacon Paperback edition in 1963
Copyright © 1963 by Beacon Press
All rights reserved
Printed in the United States of America
Beacon Press books are published under the auspices of the Unitarian
Universalist Association

International Standard Book Number: 0–8070–4671–X

9 8

Contents

Translator's Note

It is an honor to be associated with the work of Professor Lévi-Strauss, and I wish to register my gratification at being invited to collaborate in even so minor a role as that of translator.

The translation was made during the tenure of a Fellowship (1961-1962) at the Center for Advanced Study in the Behavioral Sciences, Stanford, California. I should like to express my grateful appreciation to the Center for the idyllic circumstances and the facilities which it provided, and to the University of Oxford for generously permitting me to enjoy them. Special thanks are due to Miss Lorene Yap for typing the manuscript, and to Mrs. Jacqueline Monfort for her help in the library.

R. N.

Merton College, Oxford

". . . The laws of logic which ultimately govern the world of the mind are, by their nature, essentially invariable; they are common not only to all periods and places but to all subjects of whatever kind, without any distinction even between those that we call the real and the chimerical; they are to be seen even in dreams. . . ."

—Comte, *Cours de Philosophie positive*, 52e Leçon.

Introduction

I

Totemism is like hysteria, in that once we are persuaded to doubt that it is possible arbitrarily to isolate certain phenomena and to group them together as diagnostic signs of an illness, or of an objective institution, the symptoms themselves vanish or appear refractory to any unifying interpretation. In the case of grand hysteria, the change is sometimes explained as an effect of a social evolution which has displaced the symbolic expression of mental troubles from the somatic to the psychic sphere. But the comparison with totemism suggests a relation of another order between scientific theories and culture, one in which the mind of the scholar himself plays as large a part as the minds of the people studied; it is as though he were seeking, consciously or unconsciously, and under the guise of scientific objectivity, to make the latter—whether mental patients or so-called "primitives"—more *different* than they really are. The vogue of hysteria and that of totemism were contemporary, arising from the same cultural conditions, and their parallel misadventures may be initially explained by a tendency, common to many branches of learning toward the close of the nineteenth century, to mark off certain human phenomena—as though they constituted a natural entity—which scholars preferred to regard as alien to their own moral universe, thus protecting the attachment which they felt toward the latter.

The first lesson of Freud's critique of Charcot's theory of hysteria lay in convincing us that there is no essential difference between states of mental health and mental illness; that the passage from one to the other involves at most a modification in certain general operations which everyone may see in himself; and that consequently the mental patient is our brother, since he is distinguished from us in nothing more than by an involu-

tion—minor in nature, contingent in form, arbitrary in definition, and temporary—of a historical development which is funda-
mentally that of every individual existence. It was more reassur-
ing to regard a mental patient as belonging to a rare and singular
species, as the objective product of external or internal deter-
minants such as heredity, alcoholism, or mental weakness.

In the same way, and so that pictorial academicism might
feel secure, El Greco could not be a normal person who was capable of rejecting certain ways of representing the world, but he had
to be afflicted by a malformation of the eyeball, and it was this
alone that was responsible for his elongated figures. In this case,
as in the other, cultural modes which, had they been accepted
as such, would have meant ascribing a particularity to other
modes to which a universal value had been attached, were assigned to the order of nature. By regarding the hysteric or the
artistic innovator as abnormal, we accorded ourselves the luxury
of believing that they did not concern us, and that they did not
put in question, by the mere fact of their existence, an accepted
social, moral, or intellectual order.

The same motives, and signs of the same course, may be
seen in the speculations which eventuated in the totemic illusion.
Admittedly, it was no longer a question of a direct recourse to
nature, though as we shall see there was frequent recourse to
"instinctive" attitudes or beliefs. But the idea of totemism made
possible a differentiation of societies which was almost as radical,
if not by relegating certain of them *into* nature (a procedure well
illustrated by the very term *Naturvölker*), at least by classing
them according to their attitude *toward* nature, as expressed by
the place assigned to man in the animal kingdom and by their
understanding or alleged ignorance of the mechanism of procreation. It was thus not by chance that Frazer amalgamated totemism and ignorance of physiological paternity: totemism assim-
ilates men to animals, and the alleged ignorance of the role of
the father in conception results in the replacement of the human
genitor by spirits closer still to natural forces. This naturalist
view offered a touchstone which allowed the savage, within
culture itself, to be isolated from civilized man.

In order to place the modes of thought of the normal, white adult man on a firm foundation and simultaneously to maintain them in their integrity, nothing could therefore be more convenient than for him to separate from himself those customs and beliefs, actually extremely heterogeneous and difficult to isolate, around which had crystallized an inert mass of ideas which would have been less inoffensive if it had been necessary to recognize their presence and their action in all cultures, including our own. Totemism is firstly the projection outside our own universe, as though by a kind of exorcism, of mental attitudes incompatible with the exigency of a discontinuity between man and nature which Christian thought has held to be essential. It was thus thought possible to validate this belief by making the inverse exigency an attribute of this "second nature," which civilized man, in the vain hope of escaping from himself as well as from nature itself, concocts from the "primitive" or "archaic" stages of his own development.

In the case of totemism, this was the more convenient in that sacrifice, an idea which remains central to the great western religions, presented a difficulty of the same type. Every sacrifice implies a solidarity of nature between officiant, god, and the thing sacrificed, whether this is an animal, a plant, or an object which is treated as though it were alive, since its destruction is meaningful only in the form of a holocaust. Thus the idea of sacrifice also bears within it the germ of a confusion with the animal, a confusion which entails the risk of being extended beyond man to the very god. In amalgamating sacrifice and totemism, a means was found of explaining the former as a survival or as a vestige of the latter, and thus of sterilizing the underlying beliefs and ridding of any impurity the idea of a living and active sacrifice, or at least by dissociating this idea to distinguish two types of sacrifice, different in origin and meaning.

II

These considerations, by first emphasizing the suspect character of the totemic hypothesis, help us to understand its singular destiny. For it expanded with an extraordinary rapidity, invading the entire field of ethnology and the history of religion. Yet we can now see that the signs presaging its downfall were almost contemporary with its period of triumph: it was already collapsing at the very moment when it seemed most secure.

In his book *L'État actuel du problème totémique* (The Present State of the Problem of Totemism)—a curious mixture of erudition, partiality, and even incomprehension, allied to unusual theoretical boldness and freedom of speculation—van Gennep wrote at the end of his preface, dated April 1919: "Totemism has already taxed the wisdom and the ingenuity of many scholars, and there are reasons to believe that it will continue to do so for many years."

The prognostication is easily explained, for it was made only a few years after the publication of Frazer's monumental work *Totemism and Exogamy,* years in which the international journal *Anthropos* had opened a permanent section on totemism which occupied an important place in each number. Nonetheless, it would have been difficult to be more mistaken. Van Gennep's book was to be the last work devoted entirely to this question, and on this count it remains indispensable. But, far from being the first stage in a continuing synthesis, it was rather the swan song of speculations on totemism. And it was along the lines laid down in Goldenweiser's first writings,[1] scornfully swept aside by van Gennep, that the unremitting effort at disintegration, which today is victorious, was to be conducted.

The year 1910 is a convenient point of departure for the present work, which was begun in 1960. It is exactly half a century since there appeared, in 1910, two works of very unequal dimensions, though in the end Goldenweiser's 110 pages were to exercise a more lasting theoretical influence than the 2,200 pages in Frazer's four volumes. At the very time when Frazer was publishing the totality of facts then known, in order to establish totemism as a system and to explain its origin, Goldenweiser contested the right to superimpose three kinds of phenomena—viz., an organization into clans, the attribution of animals and plants to the clans as names or emblems, and the belief in a relation between clan and animal—when in fact their contours coincide in only a minority of cases and each may be present without the others.

Thus the Thompson River Indians have totems but no clans; the Iroquois have clans called after animals which are not totems; and the Yukhagir, who are divided into clans, have religious beliefs in which animals play a large part, but through the mediation of shamans, not social groups. The supposed totemism eludes all effort at absolute definition. It consists, at most, in a contingent arrangement of nonspecific elements. It is a combination of particulars which may be empirically observable in a certain number of cases without there resulting any special properties; it is not an organic synthesis, an object in social nature.

The place assigned to totemism in American textbooks after Goldenweiser's criticisms continued to diminish with the passage of the years. In Lowie's *Primitive Society,* eight pages are still reserved for totemism, firstly to condemn Frazer's undertaking, then to sum up and support Goldenweiser's first ideas (with the reservation, nevertheless, that his definition of totemism as the "socialization of emotional values" is too ambitious and too general; for while the natives of Buin have a quasi-religious attitude toward their totems, those of the Kariera of western Australia are subject to no tabu and are not venerated). But Lowie reproaches Goldenweiser mainly for going back on his scepticism, to a certain extent, in admitting an empirical connection between totemism and clans; whereas the Crow, Hidatsa, Gros-Ventre, and Apache have clans without totemic names, and the Aranda have totemic groups which are distinct from their clans. Lowie therefore concludes: "I am not convinced that all the acumen and erudition lavished upon the subject has established the reality of the totemic phenomenon." [2]

Thereafter, the liquidation was accelerated. Let us just compare the two editions of Kroeber's *Anthropology.* That of 1923 still contains numerous references to the topic, but the problem is not examined otherwise than to distinguish clans and moieties as a method of social organization from totemism as a symbolic system. There is no necessary connection between the two, but at most a factual connection which poses an unsolved problem. And in spite of the 856 pages of the second edition, the index—though it runs to 39 pages—contains no more than a solitary entry under "Totemism," and this only to an incidental observation concerning a small tribe in Brazil, the Canella: "The second pair of moieties . . . is not concerned with marriage but is totemic—that is, certain animals or natural objects are symbolically representative of each moiety." [3]

To return to Lowie, in *An Introduction to Cultural Anthropology* (1934) he discusses totemism in half a page, and in his second textbook on primitive sociology, *Social Organization* (1948), he mentions the word "totemism" only once, and in passing, to explain Schmidt's position.

In 1938, Boas published *General Anthropology*, a textbook of 718 pages which he brought out in collaboration with his pupils. The discussion of totemism occupies four pages, written by Gladys Reichard. A number of heterogeneous phenomena, she observes, have been brought together under the name of totemism: lists of names or emblems, the belief in a supernatural relationship with non-human beings, prohibitions which may be alimentary but are not always such (e.g., to walk on grass and eat out of a bowl, in Santa Cruz; to touch a bison horn or foetus, charcoal or verdigris, insects and vermin, among the Omaha), and certain rules of exogamy. These phenomena are sometimes associated with kin groups, sometimes with military or religious fraternities, sometimes with individuals. To sum up:

> Too much has been written of totemism in its different aspects . . . to permit leaving it entirely out of the discussion. . . . Since the manifestations are so varied in different parts of the world, since their resemblances are only apparent, and since they are phenomena which may occur in many settings not related to real or supposed consanguinity, they can by no means be fitted into a single category.[4]

In his *Social Structure*, Murdock excuses himself for not dealing with the question of totemism, remarking that its bearing on the formal structuring of social relations is comparatively slight: "If social groups are to receive names, animal designations are as obvious as any." [5]

A curious study by Linton certainly contributed to the increasing indifference of American scholars toward a problem which had hitherto been so much debated. During the First World War, Linton belonged to the 42nd or "Rainbow" Division, a name arbitrarily chosen by a staff officer because the division was composed of units from so many states that their regimental colors were as varied as those of the rainbow. But as soon as the division arrived in France this name became current usage: when soldiers were asked to which unit they belonged, they would answer, "I am a Rainbow."

Around February 1918, i.e., five or six months after the division had been given this name, it was generally agreed that the appearance of a rainbow was a happy omen for it. Three months later, it was said that a rainbow was seen—even in spite of incompatible meteorological conditions—every time the division went into action.

In May 1918 the division found itself deployed near the 77th, which painted its vehicles with its own distinctive emblem, the Statue of Liberty. The Rainbow Division adopted this custom, which it thus imitated from its neighbor, but with the intention also of distinguishing itself from it. By August or September, wearing a badge in the form of a rainbow had become general, in spite of the belief that the wearing of distinctive insignia had its origin in a punishment inflicted on a defeated unit. This went on until at the end of the war the American Expeditionary Force was organized into "a series of well-defined and often mutually jealous groups, each of which had its individual complex of ideas and observances." These the author enumerates as: (1) segmentation into groups conscious of their identity; (2) the bearing by each group of the name of an animal, thing, or natural phenomenon; (3) the use of this name as term of address in conversation with strangers; (4) the use of an emblem, drawn on divisional weapons and vehicles, or as personal ornament, with a corresponding tabu on the use of the emblem by other groups; (5) respect for the "patron" and the design representing it; (6) a vague belief in its protective role and in its value as augury.

Almost any investigator who found such a condition existing among an uncivilized people would class these associated beliefs and practices as a totemic complex. It shows a poverty of content when contrasted with the highly developed totemism of the Australians or Melanesians, but it is fully as rich as the totemic complexes of some of the North American Indian tribes. The main points in which it differs from true totemism are the absence of marriage regulations, or beliefs in descent from, or of blood relationship with, the totem. . . . [6]

However, remarks Linton in conclusion, these regulations are a function of clan organization rather than of totemism properly speaking, since they do not always accompany it.

III

All the criticisms listed so far have been American, not because we accord a special place to American anthropology, but because it is a historical fact that the demolition of the problem of totemism began in the United States (despite a few prophetic pages by Tylor, never taken up, to which we shall return below), and that it was tenaciously prosecuted there. To be convinced that this was not a merely local development, we need only consider rapidly the development of ideas in England.

In 1914, one of the most famous theoretical writers on totemism, W. H. R. Rivers, defined it by the coalescence of three elements: (1) a social element, viz., the connection of an animal or vegetable species, or an inanimate object, or perhaps a class of inanimate objects, with a group defined by the society, typically with an exogamous group or clan; (2) a psychological element, viz., a belief in a relation of kinship between members of the group and the animal, plant, or thing, often expressed in the idea that the human group is descended from it; (3) a ritual element, viz., a respect for the animal, plant, or thing, typically manifested in a prohibition on eating the animal or plant, or on using the object, except on certain conditions.[7]

As the ideas of contemporary English anthropologists will be analyzed and discussed below, let us merely compare two modern views with that of Rivers. First, a current textbook:

It will be seen that the term "totemism" has been applied to a bewildering variety of relationships between human beings and natural species or phenomena. For this reason it is impossible to reach any satisfactory definition of totemism, though many attempts have been made to do so. . . . All definitions of totemism are either so specific as to exclude a number of systems which are commonly referred to as "totemic" or so general as to include many phenomena which cannot properly be referred to by this term.[8]

Second, the most recent consensus, as expressed in the sixth edition (1951) of *Notes and Queries on Anthropology*, a collective work published by the Royal Anthropological Institute:

In the widest sense of the term, we may speak of totemism if: (1) the tribe or group . . . consists of groups (totem-groups) comprising the whole population, and each of these groups has a certain relationship to a class of object (totem), animate or inanimate; (2) the relations between the social groups and the objects are of the same general kind; and (3) a member of these totemic groups cannot (except under special circumstances, such as adoption) change his membership.

Three subsidiary conditions are appended to this definition:

Totem relationship implies that every member of the species shares the totemic relationship with every member of the totem group. As a rule members of a totem group may not intermarry.

There are often obligatory rules of behavior . . . sometimes the prohibition on eating the totem species, sometimes special terms of address, decoration or badges, and a prescribed behavior to the totemic objects.[9]

This definition is more complex and precise than that of Rivers, though both of them comprise three points. But the three points of *Notes and Queries* differ from those of Rivers. His second point (belief in a relation of kinship with the totem) has disappeared; and his first and third points (connection between natural class and "typically" exogamous group, food tabu as the "typical" form of respect) are relegated, in company with other circumstances, to subsidiary conditions. In their stead, *Notes and Queries* lists: the existence of a double series in native thought, one "natural," the other social; homology of relations between terms of the two series; and the constancy of these relations. In other words, nothing remains of totemism, to which Rivers wished to give a *content*, other than a *form*:

> The term totemism is used for a form of social organization and magico-religious practice, of which the central feature is the association of certain groups (usually clans or lineages) within a tribe with certain classes of animate or inanimate things, the several groups being associated with distinct classes.[10]

But this caution with regard to a notion which can be retained only after it has been emptied of its substance and, as it were, disincarnated, does no more than underline the point of Lowie's general warning to the inventors of institutions:

> We must first inquire whether . . . we are comparing cultural realities, or merely figments of our logical modes of classification.[11]

IV

The passage from a concrete to a formal definition of totemism actually goes back to Boas. As early as 1916, aiming at Durkheim as much as at Frazer, he denied that cultural phenomena could be brought together into a unity. The notion of "myth" is a category of our thought which we use arbitrarily in order to bring together under one word attempts to explain natural phenomena, products of oral literature, philosophical speculations, and cases where linguistic processes emerged to full consciousness. Similarly, totemism is an artificial unity, existing solely in the mind of the anthropologist, to which nothing specifically corresponds in reality.

When we speak of totemism we actually confuse two problems. The first problem is that posed by the frequent identification of human beings with plants or animals, and which has to do with very general views of the relations between man and nature, relations which concern art and magic as much as society and religion. The second problem is that of the designation of groups based on kinship, which may be done with the aid of animal or vegetable terms but also in many other ways. The term "totemism" covers only cases in which there is a coincidence of the two orders.

In certain societies a very general tendency to postulate intimate connections between man and natural beings or objects is put into effect in order to qualify concretely classes of relatives, either true or classificatory. In order that such classes shall persist in a distinct and lasting form, it is necessary that these societies possess stable rules of marriage. It may therefore be affirmed that the alleged totemism always presupposes certain forms of exogamy. Van Gennep has misinterpreted Boas on this point: the latter restricts himself to affirming the logical and historical priority of exogamy over totemism, without claiming that the second is the result or a consequence of the former.

Exogamy itself can be conceived and practiced in two ways. The Eskimo restrict the exogamous unit to the family, defined by real relations of kinship. The content of each unit being strictly fixed, demographic expansion entails the creation of new units. The groups are static; since their extent is limited by definition, they are not capable of a wider integration, and they exist only on condition that, as it were, they throw people out. This form of exogamy is incompatible with totemism, because the societies which apply it lack—at least on this level—any formal structure.

If, on the contrary, the exogamous group is capable of extension, the form of the groups remains constant: it is the contents of each which increase. It becomes impossible to define membership in a group directly by genealogical means. Hence the necessity of:

(1) an unequivocal rule of descent, such as unilineal descent;

(2) a name, or at least a differentiating mark, transmitted by descent, which takes the place of a knowledge of real links.

As a general rule, there will be a progressive diminution in the number of component groups in societies of the latter type, since demographic evolution leads to the extinction of some of them. In the absence of an institutional mechanism permitting the fission of expanding groups, such as will re-establish equilibrium, this evolution will result in societies reduced to two exogamous groups. This may be one of the origins of so-called dual organizations.

On the other hand, differentiating marks in any society, though varying one from the other in content, must be formally of the same type. Otherwise, one group would be defined by name, another by ritual, another by coat of arms, and so on. However, there do exist cases of this kind, though they are rare, which demonstrate that Boas did not carry his criticism far enough. But he was certainly on the right path when he concluded that "The homology of distinguishing marks of social divisions of a tribe is proof that they are due to a classificatory tendency." [12]

In sum, Boas's thesis, which van Gennep misinterpreted, comes down to the suggestion that the formation of a system, on the social level, is a necessary condition of totemism. This is the reason that it excludes the Eskimo, whose social organization is nonsystematic, and that it necessitates unilineal descent (to which we may add bilineal descent, which is a compound development of the former, though often mistakenly confused with undifferentiated descent) because this alone is structural.

That the system should have recourse to animal and vegetable names is a particular case of a method of differential designation, the nature of which remains the same whatever the type of denotation employed.

This is perhaps where Boas's formalism misses the mark, for if the things denoted must, as he says, constitute a system, the mode of designation, in order to play its integral part, must also be systematic. The rule of homology, formulated by him, is too abstract and too hollow to meet this demand. Societies are known which do not comply with it, and it is not thereby excluded that the more complex means of differentiation which they employ shall also form a system. Conversely, the question arises why the animal and vegetable domains should offer a specially favorable nomenclature for denoting a social system, and what relations exist logically between the system of denotation and the system that is denoted. The animal world and that of plant life are not utilized merely because they are there, but because they suggest a mode of thought. The connection between the *relation of man to nature* and the *characterization of social groups,* which Boas thought to be contingent and arbitrary, only seems so because the real link between the two orders is indirect, passing through the mind. This postulates a homology, not so much within the system of denotation, but between differential features existing, on the one hand, between species *x* and *y*, and on the other, between clan *a* and clan *b.*

It is well known that the inventor of totemism as a theoretical topic was McLennan, in his *Fortnightly Review* articles called "The Worship of Animals and Plants," where is found the famous formula: totemism is fetishism plus exogamy and matrilineal descent. But hardly thirty years were required before the formulation not only of criticism in Boas's very terms, but also of developments such as we have sketched out at the end of the preceding paragraph. In 1899, namely, Tylor published ten pages on totemism, and his "remarks" could have obviated many divagations, both old and recent, if they had not been so much out of fashion. Well before Boas, Tylor suggested that in evaluating the place of totemism, "it is necessary to consider the tendency of mankind to classify out the universe." [13]

From this point of view, totemism may be defined as the association of an animal species and a human clan. But, Tylor continues,

What I venture to protest against is the manner in which totems have been placed almost at the foundation of religion. Totemism, taken up as it was as a side-issue out of the history of law, and considered with insufficient reference to the immense framework of early religion, has been exaggerated out of proportion to its real theological magnitude.[14]

And he concludes:

It may be best to postpone [certain] inquiries until . . . the totem has shrunk to the dimensions it is justly entitled to in the theological schemes of the world. Nor do I propose to enter into detailed discussion of the social results on the strength of which totemism claims a far greater importance in sociology than in religion . . . Exogamy can and does exist without totemism . . . but the frequency of their close combination over three-quarters of the earth points to the ancient and powerful action of the totems at once in consolidating clans and allying them together within the larger circle of the tribe.[15]

Which is one way of posing the problem of the logical power of systems of denotation that are borrowed from the realm of nature.

ONE

The Totemic Illusion

I

To accept as a theme for discussion a category that one believes to be false always entails the risk, simply by the attention that is paid to it, of entertaining some illusion about its reality. In order to come to grips with an imprecise obstacle one emphasizes contours where all one really wants is to demonstrate their insubstantiality, for in attacking an ill-founded theory the critic begins by paying it a kind of respect. The phantom which is imprudently summoned up, in the hope of exorcising it for good, vanishes only to reappear, and closer than one imagines to the place where it was at first.

Perhaps it would be wiser to let obsolete theories fall into oblivion, and not to awake the dead. But, as old King Arkel says, history does not produce useless events.* If great minds were fascinated for years by a problem which today seems unreal, it is because they vaguely perceived that certain phenomena, arbitrarily grouped and ill analyzed though they may have been, were nevertheless worthy of interest. How could we hope to tackle them for ourselves, in order to propose a different interpretation, without first agreeing to retread pace by pace an itinerary which, even if it led nowhere, induces us to look for another route and may help us to find it?

It should be emphasized that we employ the term totemism, sceptical though we are as to the reality of what it denotes, as it has been understood by the authors whose theories we are about to discuss. It would be inconvenient to put it always in quotation

---

* M. Maeterlinck, *Pelléas et Mélisande*, Act I, Scene 2 (Orchestra score, Paris, Durand & Cie., p. 38).

marks, or to prefix it with the word "so-called." The requirements of the argument authorize certain concessions of vocabulary. But the quotation marks and the adjective should always be understood as implicit, and a reader would be ill advised to raise objection on the ground of any phrase or expression which might appear to contradict this plainly declared position.

So much made clear, let us try to define objectively and in its most general aspects the semantic field within which are found the phenomena commonly grouped under the name of totemism.

The method we adopt, in this case as in others, consists in the following operations:

(1) define the phenomenon under study as a relation between two or more terms, real or supposed;

(2) construct a table of possible permutations between these terms;

(3) take this table as the general object of analysis which, at this level only, can yield necessary connections, the empirical phenomenon considered at the beginning being only one possible combination among others, the complete system of which must be reconstructed beforehand.

The term totemism covers relations, posed ideologically, between two series, one *natural*, the other *cultural*. The natural series comprises on the one hand *categories*, on the other *particulars*; the cultural series comprises *groups* and *persons*. All these terms are arbitrarily chosen in order to distinguish, in each series, two modes of existence, collective and individual, and in order not to confuse the series with each other. But at this preliminary stage any terms at all could be used, provided they were distinct.

NATURE . . .	Category	Particular
CULTURE . . .	Group	Person

There are four ways of associating the terms, two by two, belonging to the different series, i.e., of satisfying with the fewest conditions the initial hypothesis that there exists a relation between the two series:

	1	2	3	4
NATURE	Category	Category	Particular	Particular
CULTURE	Group	Person	Person	Group

To each of these four combinations there correspond observable phenomena among one or more peoples. Australian totemism, under "social" and "sexual" modalities, postulates a relation between a natural category (animal or vegetable species, or class of objects or phenomena) and a cultural group (moiety, section, sub-section, cult-group, or the collectivity of members of the same sex). The second combination corresponds to the "individual" totemism of the North American Indians, among whom an individual seeks by means of physical trials to reconcile himself with a natural category. As an example of the third combination we may take Mota, in the Banks Islands, where a child is thought to be the incarnation of an animal or plant found or eaten by the mother when she first became aware that she was pregnant; and to this may be added the example of certain tribes of the Algonquin group, who believe that a special relation is established between the newborn child and whatever animal is seen to approach the family cabin. The group-particular combination is attested from Polynesia and Africa, where certain animals (guardian lizards in New Zealand, sacred crocodiles and lion or leopard in Africa) are objects of social protection and veneration; it is probable that the ancient Egyptians possessed beliefs of the same type, and to such also may be related the *ongon* of Siberia, even though there they concern not real animals but figures treated by the group as though they were alive.

Logically speaking, the four combinations are equivalent, since they are all the results of the same operation. But only the first two have been included in the sphere of totemism (and it is still debated, moreover, which of the two is original, and which derivative), while the other two have been only indirectly related to totemism, one as a preliminary form (which is how Frazer regarded Mota) and the other as a vestige. Many authors even prefer to leave them completely out of account.

The totemic illusion is thus the result, in the first place, of a distortion of a semantic field to which belong phenomena of the same type. Certain aspects of this field have been singled out at the expense of others, giving them an originality and a strangeness which they do not really possess; for they are made to appear mysterious by the very fact of abstracting them from the system of which, as transformations, they formed an integral part. Are they distinguished, at least, by a greater "presence" and coherence than the other aspects? We have only to consider some examples, beginning with that which is at the origin of all speculations on totemism, to be convinced that their apparent significance is due to a mistaken division of reality.

II

It is well known that the word *totem* is taken from the Ojibwa, an Algonquin language of the region to the north of the Great Lakes of northern America. The expression *ototeman*, which means roughly, "he is a relative of mine," is composed of: initial *o-*, third person prefix; *-t-*, epenthesis serving to prevent the coalescence of vowels; *-m-*, possessive; *-an*, third person suffix; and, lastly, *-ote-*, which expresses the relationship between Ego and a male or female relative, thus defining the exogamous group at the level of the generation of the subject. It was in this way that clan membership was expressed: *makwa nindotem*, "my clan is the bear"; *pindiken nindotem*, "come in, clan-brother," etc. The Ojibwa clans mostly have animal names, a fact which Thavenet—a French missionary who lived in Canada at the end of the eighteenth century and the beginning of the nineteenth —explained by the memory preserved by each clan of an animal in its country of origin, as the most handsome, most friendly, most fearsome, or most common, or else the animal usually hunted.[1]

This collective naming system is not to be confused with the belief, held by the same Ojibwa, that an individual may enter into a relationship with an animal which will be his guardian spirit. The only known term designating this individual guardian spirit was transcribed by a traveler in the middle of the nineteenth century as *nigouimes*, and thus has nothing to do with the word "totem" or any other term of the same type. Researches on the Ojibwa show that the first description of the supposed institution of "totemism"—due to the English trader and interpreter Long, at the end of the eighteenth century—resulted from a confusion between clan-names (in which the names of animals correspond to collective appellations) and beliefs concerning guardian spirits (which are individual protectors).[2] This is more clearly seen from an analysis of Ojibwa society.

These Indians were, it seems, organized into some dozens of patrilineal and patrilocal clans, of which five may have been older than the others, or, at any rate, enjoyed a particular prestige.

A myth explains that these five "original" clans are descended from six anthropomorphic supernatural beings who emerged from the ocean to mingle with human beings. One of them had his eyes covered and dared not look at the Indians, though he showed the greatest anxiety to do so. At last he could no longer restrain his curiosity, and on one occasion he partially lifted his veil, and his eye fell on the form of a human being, who instantly fell dead "as if struck by one of the thunderers." Though the intentions of this dread being were friendly to men, yet the glance of his eye was too strong, and it inflicted certain death. His fellows therefore caused him to return to the bosom of the great water. The five others remained among the Indians, and "became a blessing to them." From them originate the five great clans or totems: catfish, crane, loon, bear, and marten.[3]

In spite of the mutilated form in which it has been handed down to us, this myth is of considerable interest. It affirms, to begin with, that there can be no direct relationship, based on contiguity, between man and totem. The only possible relationship must be "masked," and thus metaphorical, as is confirmed by the fact, reported from Australia and America, that the totemic animal is sometimes designated by another name than that applied to the real animal, to the extent that the clan name does not immediately and normally arouse a zoological or botanical association in the native mind.

In the second place, the myth establishes another opposition, between personal relation and collective relation. The

Indian does not die just because he is looked at, but also because of the singular behavior of one of the supernatural beings, whereas the others act with more discretion, and as a group.

In this double sense the totemic relationship is implicitly distinguished from that with the guardian spirit, which involves a direct contact crowning an individual and solitary quest. It is thus native theory itself, as it is expressed in the myth, which invites us to separate collective totems from individual guardian spirits, and to stress the mediating and metaphorical character of the relationship between man and the eponym of his clan. Lastly, it puts us on our guard against the temptation to construct a totemic system by accumulating relationships taken one by one, and uniting in each case *one* group of men to *one* animal species, whereas the primitive relation is between two systems: one based on distinction between groups, the other on distinction between species, in such a fashion that a plurality of groups on the one hand, and a plurality of species on the other, are placed directly in correlation and in opposition.

According to the reports by Warren, who was himself an Ojibwa, the principal clans gave birth to others:

Catfish: merman, sturgeon, pike, whitefish, sucker
Crane: eagle
Loon: cormorant, goose
Bear: ———
Marten: moose, reindeer

In 1925 Michelson recorded the following clans: marten, loon, eagle, bull-head salmon, bear, sturgeon, great lynx, lynx, crane, chicken. Some years later, and in another region (Old Desert Lake), Kinietz found six clans: water-spirit, bear, cat-fish, eagle, marten, chicken. He added to this list two more clans which had recently disappeared: crane, and an undetermined bird.

Among the eastern Ojibwa of Parry Island (in Georgian Bay, part of Lake Huron), Jenness compiled in 1929 a series of "bird" clans: crane, loon, eagle, gull, sparrowhawk, crow; a series of "animal" clans: bear, caribou, moose, wolf, beaver, otter, raccoon, skunk; a series of "fish" clans: sturgeon, pike, cat-fish. There was also another clan, waxing moon, and a whole list of names of clans which were hypothetical or which had disappeared from the region: squirrel, tortoise, marten, fisher, mink, birch-bark. The still existing clans were reduced to six: reindeer, beaver, otter, loon, falcon, and sparrowhawk.

It is also possible that the division was into five groups, by sub-division of the birds into "celestial" (eagle, sparrowhawk) and "aquatic" (all the others), and the mammals into "terrestrial" and "aquatic" (those inhabiting swampy zones, such as the cervidae of Canada, or which live on fish, such as the fisher, mink, etc.).

However this may be, it has never been reported of the Ojibwa that they believe members of a clan to be descended from the totemic animal; and the latter was not the object of a cult. Thus Landes remarks that although the caribou has completely disappeared from southern Canada, this fact did not at all worry the members of the clan named after it: "It's only a name," they said to the investigator. The totem was freely killed and eaten, with certain ritual precautions, viz., that permission had first to be asked of the animal, and apologies be made to it afterwards. The Ojibwa even said that the animal offered itself more willingly to the arrows of hunters of its own clan, and that it paid therefore to call out the name of the "totem" before shooting at it.

The chicken and the pig—creatures of European importation—were used in order to attribute a conventional clan to the half-caste offspring of Indian women and white men (because the rule of patrilineal descent would otherwise have deprived them of a clan). Sometimes such persons were also assigned to the eagle clan, because this bird figures on the arms of the United States, well known from its currency. The clans were themselves divided into bands designated by the parts of the clan animal, e.g., head, hindquarters, subcutaneous fat, etc.

In thus assembling and comparing the evidence from several regions (each of which furnishes only a partial list, since the clans are not equally represented everywhere), we may discern a tripartite division: *water* (water spirit, cat-fish, pike, sucker, sturgeon, salmonidae, and so on, i.e., all the "fish" clans); *air* (eagle, sparrowhawk, then crane, loon, gull, cormorant, goose, etc.); *earth* (first the group consisting of caribou, moose, reindeer, marten, beaver, raccoon, then that of fisher, mink, skunk, squirrel, and lastly bear, wolf, and lynx). The place of the snake and of the tortoise is uncertain.

Entirely distinct from the system of totemic names, which is governed by a principle of equivalence, there is that of the "spirits" or *manido,* which are ordered in a hierarchized pantheon. There was certainly a hierarchy of clans among the Algonquin, but this did not rest on a superiority or inferiority attributed to the eponymous animals other than in jokes such as, "My totem is the wolf, yours is the pig. . . . Take care! Wolves eat pigs!" [4] At most there were reported hints of physical and moral distinctions, conceived of as specific properties. The system of "spirits," to the contrary, was plainly ordered along two axes: that of greater and lesser spirits, and that of beneficent and maleficent spirits. At the summit, the great spirit; then his servants; then, in descending order—both morally and physically—the sun and moon, forty-eight thunderers opposed to mythical snakes, "little invisible Indians," male and female water spirits, the four cardinal points, and finally hordes of *manido,* named and unnamed, which haunt the sky, the earth, the waters, and the chthonian world. In a sense, therefore, the two systems—"totems" and *manido*—are at right angles to each other, one being approximately horizontal, the other vertical, and they coincide at only one point, since the water spirits alone are unambiguously present in both the one and the other. This may perhaps explain why the supernatural spirits in the myth related above, who are responsible for the totemic names and for the division into clans, are described as emerging from the ocean.

All the food tabus reported from the Ojibwa derive from the *manido* system, and they are all explained in the same way, viz., as prohibitions communicated to the individual in dreams, on the part of particular spirits, against eating a certain meat or a certain part of the body of an animal, e.g., the flesh of the porcupine, the tongue of the moose, etc. The animal concerned does not necessarily figure in the list of clan names.

	MANIDO	SYSTEM
	great	spirit
	sun	moon
	thun-	derers
	cardinal	points
"TOTEMIC" SYSTEM	eagle, goose, water	spirits, pike, sturgeon, etc.
	chthonian	snakes
	et	c.

Similarly, the acquisition of a guardian spirit came as the consummation of a strictly individual enterprise which girls and boys were encouraged to undertake when they approached puberty. If they succeeded they gained a supernatural protector whose characteristics and circumstances of appearance were signs informing the candidates of their aptitudes and their vocations. These favors were only granted, however, on condition of behaving with obedience and considerateness toward the protector. In spite of all these differences, the confusion between totem and guardian spirit into which Long fell may be explained in part by the fact that the latter was never "a particular mammal or bird, such as one might see by day around the wigwam, but a supernatural being which represented the entire species." [5]

III

Let us now look at another part of the world, described by Raymond Firth in accounts which have contributed greatly to the exposure of the extreme complexity and heterogeneous character of beliefs and customs too hastily lumped together under the label of totemism. These analyses are all the more illuminating in that they concern a region—Tikopia—which Rivers thought to furnish the best proof of the existence of totemism in Polynesia.

But, says Firth, before advancing such a view:

. . . it is essential to know whether on the human side the relation [with the species or natural object] is one in which people are involved as a group or only as individuals, and, as regards the animal or plant, whether each species is concerned as a whole or single members of it alone are considered; whether the natural object is regarded as a representative or emblem of the human group; whether there is any idea of identity between a person and the creature or object and of descent of one from the other; and whether the interest of the people is focused on the animal or plant *per se,* or it is of importance primarily through a belief in its association with ancestral spirits or other deities. And in the latter event it is very necessary to understand something of the native concept of the relation between the species and the supernatural being.[6]

This suggests that to the two axes which we have distinguished, viz., *group-individual* and *nature-culture,* a third should be added on which should be arranged the different conceivable types of relation between the extreme terms of the first two axes: emblematic, relations of identity, descent, or interest, direct, indirect, etc.

Tikopia society is composed of four patrilineal but not necessarily exogamous groups called *kainanga,* each headed by a chief (*ariki*) who stands in a special relationship to the *atua.* This latter term designates gods properly speaking, as well as ancestral spirits, the souls of former chiefs, etc. As for the native conception of nature, this is dominated by a fundamental distinction between "edible things" (*e kai*) and "inedible things" (*sise e kai*).

The "edible things" consist mainly of vegetables and fish. Among the vegetables, four species are of first importance in that each has a particular affinity with one of the four clans: the yam "listens to" or "obeys" *sa Kafika;* and the same relation obtains between the coconut and the clan *sa Tafua,* the taro and the clan *sa Taumako,* the breadfruit and the clan *sa Fangarere.* In fact, the vegetable is thought to belong directly, as in the Marquesas, to the clan god (incarnated in one of the numerous varieties of freshwater eels or those of the coastal reefs), and the agricultural rite primarily takes the form of a solicitation of the god. The role of a clan chief is thus above all to "control" a vegetable species. A further distinction between species is necessary: the planting and harvesting of the yam or taro, and the harvest of the breadfruit tree, are of a seasonal nature. This is not the case with coconut palms, which reproduce spontaneously, and the nuts of which ripen all year round. This difference may perhaps correspond to that between the respective forms of control: everybody possesses, cultivates, and harvests the first three species, and prepares and consumes their products, while only the clan in charge of them performs the ritual. But there is no special ritual for coconut palms, and the clan which controls them, Tafua, is subject to only a few tabus: in order to drink the milk, its members have to pierce the shell instead of breaking it; and in order to open the nuts and extract the flesh they may use only a stone, and no other tool.

These differential modes of conduct are not interesting solely because of the correlation they suggest between rites and beliefs on the one hand and certain objective conditions on the other. They also support the criticism advanced above against the rule of homology formulated by Boas, since three clans express their relationship to the natural species through ritual, and the fourth through prohibitions and prescriptions. The homology, therefore, if it exists, has to be sought at a deeper level.

However this may be, it is clear that the relationship of men to certain vegetable species is expressed under two aspects, sociological and religious. As among the Ojibwa, a myth is resorted to in order to unify them:

A long time ago the gods were no different from mortals, and the gods were the direct representatives of the clans in the land. It came about that a god from foreign parts, Tikarau, paid a visit to Tikopia, and he gods of the land prepared a splendid feast for him, but first they organized trials of strength or speed, to see whether their guest or they would win. During a race, the stranger slipped and declared that he was injured. Suddenly, however, while he was pretending to limp, he made a dash for the provisions for the feast, grabbed up the heap, and fled for the hills. The family of gods set off in pursuit; Tikarau slipped and fell again, so that the clan gods were able to retrieve some of the provisions, one a coconut, another a taro, another a bread-fruit, and others a yam. Tikarau succeeded in reaching the sky with most of the foodstuffs for the feast, but these four vegetable foods had been saved for men.[7]

Different though it is from that of the Ojibwa, this myth has several points in common with it which need to be em-phasized. Firstly, the same opposition will be noted between in-dividual and collective conduct, the former being negatively re-garded and the latter positively in relation to totemism. In the two myths, the individual and maleficent conduct is that of a greedy and inconsiderate god (a point on which there are re-semblances with Loki of Scandinavia, of whom a masterly study has been made by Georges Dumézil). In both cases, totemism as a system is introduced as *what remains* of a diminished totality, a fact which may be a way of expressing that the terms of the system are significant only if they are *separated* from each other, since they alone remain to equip a semantic field which was previously better supplied and into which a discontinuity has been introduced. Finally, the two myths suggest that direct contact (between totemic gods and men in one case; gods in the form of men and totems in the other), i.e., a relation of con-tiguity, is contrary to the spirit of the institution: the totem be-comes such only on condition that it first be set apart.

On Tikopia, the category of "edible things" also includes fish. However, there is no direct association at all between the clans and edible fish. The question is complicated when the gods are brought into the picture. On the one hand, the four vegetable foods are held to be sacred because they "represent" the gods—

the yam is the "body" of the deity Kafika, the taro is that of Taumako; the breadfruit and coconut are respectively the "head" of Fangarere and of Tafua—but, on the other hand, the gods "are" fish, particularly eels. We thus rediscover, in a transposed form, the distinction between totemism and religion which has already been discerned in the opposition between resemblance and contiguity. As among the Ojibwa, Tikopian totemism is expressed by means of metaphorical relations.

On the religious plane, however, the relation between god and animal is of a metonymic order, firstly because the *atua* is believed to *enter* the animal, but does not change into it; secondly because it is never the *totality* of the species that is in question but only a single animal (therefore a *part* of the species) which is recognized, by its unusual behavior, as being the vehicle of a god; lastly because this kind of occurrence takes place only intermittently and even exceptionally, while the more distant relation between vegetable species and god is of a more permanent nature. From this last point of view, one might almost say that metonymy corresponds to the order of events, metaphor to the order of structure.[8]*

That the plants and edible animals are not themselves gods is confirmed by another fundamental opposition, that between *atua* and food. It is in fact inedible fish, insects, and reptiles that are called *atua*, probably, as Firth suggests, because "creatures which are unfit for human consumption are not of the normal order of nature. . . . [In the case of animals] it is not the edible, but the inedible elements which are associated with supernatural beings." If, then, Firth continues, "we are to speak . . . of these phenomena as constituting totemism it must be acknowledged that there are in Tikopia two distinct types of the institution— the positive, relating to plant food-stuffs, with emphasis on fertility; the negative, relating to animals, with emphasis on unsuitability for food." [9]

* Seen in this perspective, the two myths of the origin of totemism which we have summarized and compared may also be considered as myths concerning the origin of metaphor. And as a metaphorical structure is, in general, characteristic of myths, they therefore constitute in themselves metaphors of the second degree.

The ambivalence attributed to animals appears even greater in that the gods assume many forms of animal incarnation. For the *sa Tafua,* the clan god is an eel which causes the coconuts of its adherents to ripen; but he can also change into a bat, and as such destroy the palm plantations of other clans. Hence the prohibition on eating bats, as well as water hens and other birds, and also fish, which stand in a particularly close relationship to certain deities. These prohibitions, which may be either general or limited to a clan or lineage, are not however of a totemic character: the pigeon, which is closely connected with Taumako clan, is not eaten, but there are no scruples against killing it, because it plunders the gardens. Moreover, the prohibition is restricted to the first-born.

Behind the particular beliefs and prohibitions there is a fundamental scheme, the formal properties of which exist independently of the relations between a certain animal or vegetable species and a certain clan, sub-clan or lineage, through which it may be discerned.

Thus the dolphin has a special affinity for the Korokoro lineage of Tafua clan. When it is stranded on the beach, members of this kin group make it an offering of fresh vegetable foodstuffs called *putu,* "offering on the grave of a person recently deceased." The meat is then cooked and shared between the clans, with the exception of the kin group in question, for which it is *tapu* because the dolphin is the preferred form of incarnation of their *atua.*

The rules of distribution assign the head to the Fangarere, the tail to the Tafua, the forepart of the body to the Taumako, and the hindpart to the Kafika. The two clans whose vegetable species (yam and taro) is a god's "body" are thus entitled to "body" parts, and the two whose species (coconut, breadfruit) is a god's "head" receive the extremities (head and tail). The form of a system of relations is thus extended, in a coherent fashion, to a situation which at first sight might appear quite foreign to it. And, as among the Ojibwa, a second system of relations with the supernatural world, entailing food prohibitions, is combined with a formal structure while at the same time remaining clearly distinct from it, though the totemic hypothesis would incline one to confuse them. The divinized species which are the objects of the prohibitions constitute a separate system from that of clan functions which are themselves related to plant foodstuffs: e.g., the octopus, which is assimilated to a mountain, the streams of which are like its tentacles, and, for the same reason, to the sun and its rays; and eels, both fresh-water and marine, which are objects of a food tabu so strong that even to see them may cause vomiting.

We may thus conclude, with Firth, that in Tikopia the animal is conceived neither as an emblem, nor as an ancestor, nor as a relative. The respect and the prohibitions connected with certain animals are explained, in a complex fashion, by the triad of ideas that the group is descended from an ancestor, that the god is incarnated in an animal, and that in mythical times there existed a relation of alliance between ancestor and god. The respect observed toward the animal is thus accorded to it indirectly.

On the other hand, attitudes toward plants and toward animals are opposed to each other. There are agricultural rites, but none for fishing or hunting. The *atua* appear to men in the form of animals, never of plants. Food tabus, when they exist, apply to animals, not plants. The relation of the gods to vegetable species is symbolic, that to animal species is real; in the case of plants it is established at the level of the species, whereas an animal species is never in itself *atua*, but only a particular animal in certain circumstances. Finally, the plants which are "marked" by differential behavior are always edible; in the case of animals the reverse obtains. Firth, in a brief comparison of Tikopian facts with the generality of Polynesian reports, expresses almost word for word the formula of Boas, drawing the lesson that totemism does not constitute a phenomenon *sui generis* but a specific instance in the general field of relations between man and the objects of his natural environment.[10]

IV

The facts reported from the Maori, which are more remote from the classical conception of totemism, link so well with those reported from Tikopia that they strengthen the argument still further. If certain lizards are respected as guardians of funerary caves and of trees in which birds are trapped, this is because the lizard represents the god Whiro, who is the personification of sickness and death. There is a relation of descent between the gods and natural elements or beings: from the union of rock and water were born all the varieties of sand, pebbles, sandstone, and other minerals (nephrite, flint, lava, slag), as well as insects, lizards, and vermin. The god and goddess Tane-nui-a-Rangui and Kahu-parauri brought forth all the birds and fruits of the forest; Rongo is the ancestor of cutivated plants, Tangaroa is that of fish, and Haumia is the ancestor of wild plants.[11]

The whole cosmos of the Maori unfolds itself as a gigantic "kin," in which heaven and earth are first parents of all beings and things, such as the sea, the sand on the beach, the wood, the birds, and man. Apparently he does not feel quite comfortable if he cannot—preferably in much detail—give an account of his kinship whether to the fish of the sea or to a traveller who is invited to enter as a guest. With real passion the high-born Maori studies the genealogies, compares them with those of his guests, tries to find common ancestors, and unravels older and younger lines. There are examples that he has kept in order genealogies including up to 1400 persons.[12]

New Zealand has never been mentioned as offering typical examples of totemism. But it constitutes a limiting case which permits the distinction, in a pure state, of categories which are mutually exclusive but which the totemic hypothesis would have to say were compatible. It is because the animals, vegetables, and minerals are genuinely thought of by the Maori as ancestors that they cannot play the part of totems. As in the "evolutionary" myths of Samoa, a series formed of elements belonging to the three great orders of nature is conceived as a continuity from a dual point of view which is at once genetic and diachronic. Now if the natural beings or elements are related to each other as ancestors to descendants, and all of them together are so related to mankind, then none is fit in itself to play the part of ancestor in relation to any particular human group. To use a modern terminology, a totemism in which the clans are considered as originating from different species must be, by this fact, polygenetic (whereas Polynesian thought is monogenetic). But this polygenesis itself possesses a very special character, since totemism, as in certain games of patience, lays all its cards on the table at the beginning of play: it has none in reserve to illustrate the stages of transition between the animal or vegetable ancestor and the human descendant. The passage from one to the other is thus necessarily conceived as discontinuous (all transitions of the same type, moreover, being simultaneous), a veritable "scene-shifting," without dropping the curtain, which excludes all perceptible contiguity between the initial and the final states. As remote as they can possibly be from the model suggested by natural genesis, totemic origins are applications, projections, or dissociations; they consist of metaphorical relations, the analysis of which belongs to an "ethno-logic" rather than an "ethno-biology:" to say that clan A is "descended" from the bear and that clan B is "descended" from the eagle is nothing more than a concrete and abbreviated way of stating the relationship between A and B as analogous to a relationship between species.

In the same way as it helps to clarify the confusion between the notions of genesis and system, so Maori ethnography permits the dissolution of another confusion (which derives from the same totemic illusion), viz., between the notion of totem and that of *mana*. The Maori define each being or type of being according to its "nature" or "norm," *tika*, and by its particular function or distinctive behavior, *tikanga*. Thus conceived under a differential aspect, things and beings are distinguished by the *tupu*, which comes to them from within and the idea of which is contrary to that of *mana*, which comes from without and thus constitutes by contrast a principle of indistinction and confusion:

Mana has a meaning which has not a little in common with *tupu*, but on a significant point they are radically different. Both denote unfolding, activity and life; but whereas *tupu* is an expression of the nature of things and human beings as unfolded from within, *mana* expresses something participated, an active fellowship which according to its nature is never inextricably bound up with any single thing or any single human being.[13]

Now the customs concerning tabus (*tapu*, not to be confused with *tupu*) are themselves also situated at the level of a discontinuity which does not justify the kind of amalgamation often attempted by Durkheim and his school between the notions of *mana*, totem, and tabu:

What makes the *tapu* customs an institution is . . . a profound respect for life, an awe in which now honour, now fear stands in the foreground. The awe does not regard life in general, but life in its various manifestations, and not even all manifestations, only life as included in the great fellowship of the kinship group as it extends into field, forest, and fishing grounds, and culminates in the chief, treasures, and sacred places.[14]

Australian Nominalism

I

In 1920 van Gennep reviewed forty-one different theories of totemism, the most important and the most recent of which were undoubtedly those erected on the basis of facts from Australia. It is not surprising, therefore, that A. P. Elkin, the eminent present-day specialist on Australia, should have resorted to the same facts in taking the problem up again, employing an empirical and descriptive method, and an analytical framework, set out several years earlier by Radcliffe-Brown.

Elkin sticks so closely to ethnographic reality that it is essential to begin by recalling certain elementary facts, without which it would be impossible to follow his argument.

A number of measurements of carbon-14 residual radioactivity have pushed the entry of man into the Australian continent back to before the eighth millennium B.C. It is no longer claimed today that the natives of Australia remained completely cut off from the external world during this enormous lapse of time: on the northern coast, at least, there must have been numerous contacts and exchanges with New Guinea (either directly or through the islands of the Torres Straits) and with southern Indonesia. However, it is probable that, relatively speaking, Australian societies have on the whole developed in isolation to a much higher degree than other societies elsewhere in the world. This accounts for the numerous features that they have in common, above all in the sphere of religion and in social organization, and the often characteristic distribution of modalities belonging to the same type.

All the societies "without classes" (i.e., without moieties, sections, or sub-sections) occupy a peripheral position, on the coasts of Dampier Land, Arnhem Land, the Gulf of Carpentaria, Cape York Peninsula, New South Wales, Victoria, and the Great Australian Bight. This distribution may be explained either by the supposition that these forms are the most archaic and have persisted as vestiges around the circumference of the continent, or—which is the more likely—that they are the result of a marginal disintegration of class-systems.

The societies with matrilineal moieties (without sections or sub-sections) occupy a vast area in the southeast (the southern part of Queensland, New South Wales, Victoria, and the eastern part of South Australia), and also a small coastal zone in the southwest of Western Australia.

The societies with patrilineal moieties (with sections or sub-sections) are found in the north of the continent, from Dampier Land as far as Cape York Peninsula.

Finally, four-section systems are found in the northwest (the desert region, and as far as the western coast) and the northeast (Queensland), and on all sides of the central region, which is occupied by eight-section systems (from Arnhem Land and Cape York Peninsula down as far as Lake Eyre in the south).

Let us sum up briefly the features of societies with "marriage classes." This is scarcely necessary for moieties, since these are defined by the simple rule that an individual belonging to one moiety (by either patrilineal or matrilineal descent, both being found in Australia) is under the obligation to take a spouse from the other moiety.

Let us now imagine two groups, living in separate territories, each being bound by the exogamous rule of its moieties, and let us further suppose that descent is matrilineal (since this is the most common case, though the inverse hypothesis would yield a parallel result). In order to unite, these two groups decide that their respective members may take their spouses only from the other group, and that a wife and her children shall reside with the father. Let us call the two matrilineal moieties Jones and Smith, and the two local groups Oxford and Cambridge. The rule of marriage will then be:

┌→ Jones of Oxford   =   Smith of Cambridge ←┐
└→ Jones of Cambridge   =   Smith of Oxford   ←┘

This is to be read as: if a Jones man of Oxford marries a Smith woman of Cambridge, the children will be Smith (after their mother) of Oxford (after their father). This is what is called the four-section system, or Kariera, after the name of a tribe in western Australia.

The transition to an eight-section system follows the same procedure, but starting with four local groups instead of two. In the following diagram of such a system the letters indicate patrilineal local groups, and the figures the matrilineal moieties. Whichever way it is read (whether from right to left or left to right), the first pair of characters represents the father, the second the mother, and the arrow joins the mother to her children (as in the Aranda system):

$$A1 \ = \ C2$$
$$B1 \ = \ D2$$
$$C1 \ = \ B2$$
$$D1 \ = \ A2$$

The rationale behind these rules has been well set out by van Gennep:

. . . the result, and probably the aim, of exogamy is to link together certain societies which without it would no more come into contact than the masons of Rouen and the hairdressers of Marseille. If we examine the marriage diagrams from this point of view . . . we see that the positive element in exogamy is quite as powerful as the negative, but that, as in all codes, only what is forbidden is specified. . . . Under its two indissociable aspects, the institution thus serves to reinforce the cohesion, not so much between members of the clan, but between different clans vis-à-vis society in general. It establishes a matrimonial interchange through the generations which is the more complicated in proportion with the age of the society and the increasing number of its segments, an interchange and alternating mingling in which exogamy ensures regularity and periodical return.[1]

This interpretation, which is also our own (see *Les Structures élémentaires de la parenté*), seems to us to be still superior to that proposed by Radcliffe-Brown in even his latest writings, viz., to derive four-section systems from a double dichotomy of matrilineal moieties (which are not to be contested) and of alternating generations of named or unnamed masculine lines. It often happens, in fact, that lines of men in Australia are divided into two categories, one comprising the even generations and the other the odd, counting from that of the subject. Thus a man will be included in the same category as his grandfather and his grandson, while his father and his son belong to the alternate category. But this classification would itself be impossible to interpret other than by seeing it as the consequence, whether direct or indirect, or the complex interplay of the rules of marriage and descent. Logically, it cannot be regarded as a prior phenomenon. On the contrary, every ordered society, whatever its organization or degree of complexity, has to be defined, in one way or another, in terms of residence; and it is therefore legitimate to have recourse instead to a particular rule of residence as a structural principle.

In the second place, an interpretation based on the dialectic of residence and descent has the immense advantage that it permits the integration of the classical Australian systems—viz., Kariera and Aranda—into a general typology leaving no so-called irregular system out of account. There would be no point in insisting on this second aspect here, because such a general typology is based exclusively on sociological features and leaves totemic beliefs and customs on one side: these have only a secondary place among the Kariera, and although the same cannot be said of the Aranda their totemic beliefs and customs, important though they are, belong to an entirely different sphere from that of the marriage rules and seem to have no influence on them.

II

The originality of Elkin's undertaking consists precisely in re-examining Australian societies from the standpoint of totemism. He proposes three criteria for the definition of a totemic system: *form,* or the way in which the totems are distributed between individuals and groups (with respect to sex, membership of a clan or moiety, etc.); *meaning,* according to the part played by the totem with respect to the individual (as helper, guardian, companion, or as symbol of the social or cult group); and, finally, *function,* corresponding to the part played by the totemic system in the group (regulation of marriage, social and moral sanctions, philosophy, etc.).

Elkin further accords a special place to two forms of totemism. "Individual" totemism is found mainly in the southeast of Australia. This form involves a relationship between a sorcerer and a certain animal species, normally a reptile. The animal lends its assistance to the sorcerer, on the one hand as a beneficent or maleficent agent, and on the other as a messenger or spy. Cases are known of the sorcerer exhibiting a tamed animal as proof of his power. This form of totemism has been reported from New South Wales, among the Kamilaroi and the Kurnai, and it is found in the Northern Territory, as far as Dampier Land, in the form of a belief in mythical snakes which live inside the body of the sorcerer. The identity postulated between totem and man entails a food tabu, since to eat the animal would amount to auto-cannibalism. More precisely, the zoological species appears as a mediating term between the soul of the species and that of the sorcerer.

"Sexual" totemism is found from the region of Lake Eyre as far as the coast of New South Wales and Victoria. The Dieri relate the sexes to two plants. Sometimes "birds" are also invoked: the bat and the owl (Dieri); bat and woodpecker (Worimi); emu-wren and superb warbler (Kurnai); wren and bat (Yuin). In all these tribes the totems listed serve as emblems of sexual groups. If a masculine or feminine totem is injured by a representative of the other sex, the entire sexual group feels insulted and a dispute between men and women ensues. This emblematic function rests on the belief that each of the sexual groups forms a living community with the animal species. As the Wotjobaluk say, "The life of a bat is a man's life." We do not know very much about how the natives interpret this affinity: whether as a belief in the reincarnation of each sex in the form of the corresponding creature, or in a relation of friendship or fraternity, or whether yet in myths in which the ancestors bear animal names.

With only a few rare exceptions, found on the coast of New South Wales and Victoria, sexual totemism seems to be associated with matrilineal moieties. Hence the hypothesis that sexual totemism may correspond to a desire to "mark off" the feminine group more strongly: among the Kurnai, women used to force the hand of men too reserved to propose marriage by killing a masculine totem; this would result in a fight, which could be ended only by the contraction of marriage. However, Roheim has found sexual totemism along the Finke River, among certain Aranda to the northwest, and among the Aluridja. Now the Aranda have patrilineal moieties of a ceremonial nature, having no connection with either local totemic cults or a "conceptional" form of totemism, to which we shall come below. However, other customs or institutions are not without similarities to those of the Kurnai. Among the Aranda as well the woman sometimes takes the initiative: normally, in order to determine the totem of her child, by herself announcing the place where conception took place; and on the occasion of specifically feminine ceremonial dances of an erotic kind. Also, among some Aranda at least, the maternal totem is respected as much as one's own.

III

The great problem of Australian totemism is that posed by its relation to the rules of marriage. We have seen that the latter—in their simplest forms—bring into play divisions of the group into moieties, sections, and sub-sections. It is extremely tempting to interpret this series in the "natural" order 2-4-8. The sections would thus result from a doubling of the moieties, and the sub-sections from a doubling of the sections. But what part may be assigned in this genetic process to structures which are totemic properly speaking? And, more generally, what relations subsist in Australian societies between social organization and religion?

In this connection, the northern Aranda have for long attracted attention, for while they possess totemic groups, local groups, and marriage classes, there exists no clear relation between these three types of structure, which seem to be placed on different levels and to function independently of each other. Contrarily, on the border of eastern Kimberley and the Northern Territory, there is reported a coalescence of social and religious structures; but, by this very fact, the former cease to ensure the regulation of marriage. There, it is as though the sub-sections, sections, and moieties were forms of totemism, and that they were just as much concerned with the ordering of man's relationships not only with society but with nature.[2] Actually, in this region the regulation of marriage is based not on membership of a group but on kinship.

Is this not the case in certain societies with sub-sections? In the eastern part of Arnhem Land the sub-sections possess distinct totems, which is to say that the rules of marriage and totemic affiliation coincide. Among the Mungarai and the Yungman of the Northern Territory and Kimberley, whose totems are associated with named localities and not with social groups, the situation is the same, thanks to the ingenious theory that foetal spirits are always careful to take up their abode in the bosom of a woman of the desired sub-section, so that the theoretical coincidence of totem with sub-section shall be respected.

The situation is quite different among the Kaitish, the northern Aranda, and the northwestern Loritja. Their totemism is "conceptional," i.e., the totem attributed to each child is no longer that of its father or mother, or of its grandfather, but that of the animal, plant, or natural phenomenon mythically associated with the locality at which (or near which) the mother felt the onset of her pregnancy. This apparently arbitrary rule is often manipulated, thanks to the care taken by the foetal spirits to choose women who are of the same sub-section as the mother of the totemic ancestor. It nonetheless happens, as Spencer and Gillin have already explained, that an Aranda child does not necessarily belong to the totemic group of either his father or his mother, and that, according to the place at which the mother chances to become aware of her condition, children born of the same parents may belong to different totems.

Consequently the existence of sub-sections is not enough to identify societies assimilated so far by this single criterion. Sometimes the sub-sections are merged with totemic groups, without affecting the regulation of marriage, which is left to determination by degree of relationship. Sometimes the sub-sections function as marriage classes, but then they no longer have any direct connection with totemic affiliation.

The same uncertainty is found in societies with sections. Sometimes the totemic system is similarly sectional, sometimes a number of totemic clans are divided into four groups corresponding to the four sections. As a section-system assigns the children to a different section than that of one or the other of the parents (in fact, the section alternates with that of the mother within the same moiety, a mode of transmission to which the name of indirect matrilineal descent has been given), the children have totems which necessarily differ from those of their parents.

The societies with moieties but neither sections nor subsections have a peripheral distribution. In northwestern Australia the moieties are named after two species of kangaroo; in the southwest, after two birds, white cockatoo and crow, or hawk and crow; and, in the east, after two varieties of cockatoo, such as black and white, etc.

This dualism is extended to the whole of nature, and therefore, theoretically at least, all beings and phenomena are divided between the two moieties: this tendency has become apparent among the Aranda, since the totems which have been recorded, numbering well over four hundred, are grouped into about sixty categories. The moieties are not necessarily exogamous, provided that the rules of exogamy—totemic, kinship, and local —are respected. Finally, the moieties may exist by themselves, as is the case in the peripheral societies, or be accompanied by sections or sub-sections or by both these forms. Thus the tribes of the Laverton region have sections but neither moieties nor sub-sections; in Arnhem Land, tribes have been reported with moieties and sub-sections but no sections. Lastly, the Nangiomeri have only sub-sections, with neither moieties nor sections. It thus appears that the moieties do not belong to a genetic series in which they constitute a necessary condition for the origin of sections (in the way that these, in their turn, might be the condition for sub-sections); that their function is not to regulate marriage, necessarily and automatically; and that their most constant characteristic lies in their connection with totemism, through the bipartition of the universe into two categories.

IV

Let us now consider the form of totemism which Elkin calls "clan totemism." Australian clans may be patrilineal or matrilineal, or else "conceptional," i.e., grouping together all individuals supposedly conceived in the same place. Whichever of these types the clans may be, they are normally totemic, i.e., their members observe prohibitions on eating one or more totems, and they have the right or the obligation to perform rites ensuring the multiplication of the totemic species. The relation uniting members of the clan with their totem is defined, according to tribe, genealogically (the totem being the ancestor of the clan) or locally (when a horde is linked to its totems through its territory, in which are found the totemic sites, places where the spirits which came from the body of the mythical ancestor are thought to live). The relationship to the totem may even be simply mythical, as in the case of section-systems in which a man belongs to the same section, within his matrilineal moiety, as his father's father, and possesses the same totems as the latter.

Matrilineal clans predominate in eastern Australia (Queensland, New South Wales), the western part of Victoria, and also in a small area in the southwest of Western Australia. From the alleged ignorance (which is more likely a denial) of the role of the father in conception, it results that the child receives from its mother one flesh and one blood, continually perpetuated in the feminine line. Members of the same clan are therefore said to be "of one flesh," and in the language of the eastern part of South Australia the same term as is used for flesh also means totem. From this carnal identification of clan and totem derive both the rule of clan exogamy, on the social level, and the food tabus, on the religious level: like must not be mixed with like, whether by eating or by copulation.

In such systems each clan generally possesses a principal totem and a very considerable number of secondary or tertiary totems, ranked in order of decreasing importance. All beings, things, and natural phenomena are comprised in a veritable system. The structure of the universe reproduces that of society.

Patrilineal clans are found in Western Australia, the Northern Territory, Cape York Peninsula, and, on the coast, on the borders of New South Wales and Queensland. Like the matrilineal clans, these clans are totemic, with the difference that each of them is merged with a local patrilineal horde, and the spiritual link with the totem is established, no longer by flesh, but locally, through totemic sites situated in the horde territory. There are two consequences of this situation, according to whether transmission of the totem is in the paternal line or whether it is "conceptional."

In the former case, patrilineal totemism adds nothing to local exogamy. Religion and social structure are in a harmonic relationship: as far as the status of individuals is concerned, they duplicate each other. This is the reverse of what we saw in the case of matrilineal clans, for since marital residence in Australia is always patrilocal the relation between rule of descent and rule of residence was then dysharmonic, their effects combining to define an individual status which was never exactly that of either parent.* Moreover, there is no connection between totemism

---

* The terms "harmonic" and "dysharmonic" are defined, and their implications examined, in *Les Structures élémentaires de la parenté.*

and the native theory of procreation. Belonging to the same totem expresses only a local phenomenon, the solidarity of the horde.

When the totem is determined by the "conceptional" method (whether, as among the Aranda, by reference to the place of conception, or, as in the western part of South Australia, by reference to the place of birth) the situation becomes more complicated. Since residence is patrilocal in this case also, there is every chance that conception and birth shall occur in the territory of the paternal horde, thus preserving an indirect patrilineal rule of transmission of totems. Nevertheless, exceptions may occur, mainly when families are on the move, and in such societies it is merely probable that the totem of the children shall still be one of those belonging to the paternal horde. The rule of totemic exogamy is not found, whether as a consequence or as a concomitant feature, among the Aranda (at least among the northern Aranda). These leave the regulation of exogamy to relations of kinship or to the system of sub-sections, which are quite independent of the totemic clans.* It is striking that, in a correlative fashion, the food tabus should be more flexible and sometimes even nonexistent (as among the Yaralde) in societies with patrilineal clans, whereas in a strict form they seem always to be associated with matrilineal clans.

We may content ourselves here by merely mentioning incidentally a last form of totemism described by Elkin, viz., "dream totemism," which is found in the northwest, among the Karadjeri, and in two regions of South Australia, among the Dieri, Macumba, and Loritja. The dream-totem may be revealed to the future mother when she feels the first symptoms of pregnancy, sometimes after eating some meat which because of its unusual fattiness is taken to have a supernatural character. The "dream" totem is distinct from the "cult" totem, which is determined by the place of birth of the child.

---

* The reports of Spencer and Gillen on this point have been challenged. (Cf. C. Lévi-Strauss, *La Pensée Sauvage,* Paris, 1962, ch. III.) For the present, it may merely be noted that even according to a modern interpretation (Elkin, 1954) Aranda institutions are still markedly different from those of their neighbors to the north and south.

After a long analysis, taken up again and completed in other works, and which we have only very briefly summed up and commented on here, Elkin concludes that there are heterogeneous forms of totemism in Australia. These may be combined: e.g., the Dieri, who live in the northwest of South Australia, possess simultaneously moiety totemism, sexual totemism, matriclan totemism, and a cult totemism linked to patrilocal residence. Moreover, among these natives the cult totem of the mother's brother is respected by the sister's son in addition to that of his father (the only one which he himself transmits to his sons). In northern Kimberley, forms of totemism defined by moiety, patrilineal local horde, and dream are found in association. The southern Aranda have patrilineal totemic cults (which are merged with dream totems) and totemic cults inherited from the mother's brother, while among other Aranda there exists individual "conceptional" totemism associated with a respect for the maternal clan.

Distinction is therefore made between irreducible "species": individual totemism; social totemism, within which are distinguished, as so many varieties, totemism by sex, moiety, section, sub-section, and clan (matrilineal or patrilineal); cult totemism, which has a religious character and of which there are two varieties, one patrilineal and the other "conceptional"; and, finally, dream totemism, which may be either social or individual.

V

As may be seen, Elkin's procedure begins as a healthy reaction against the imprudent or excessive amalgams to which theoreticians of totemism have had recourse in order to establish totemism as a unique institution recurring in a great number of societies. It is not to be doubted that the immense effort of investigation undertaken by Australian anthropologists, following Radcliffe-Brown, remains an indispensable basis for any new interpretation of the Australian facts. But without at all withholding from one of the most fertile contemporary schools of anthropology, or from its head, the admiration to which they are entitled, it may be wondered whether the latter has not allowed himself to be trapped, theoretically as well as methodologically, by a dilemma which was by no means unavoidable.

Although his study is presented in an objective and empirical form, it seems that Elkin undertakes a reconstruction in a field devastated by American criticism. His attitude toward Radcliffe-Brown is more equivocal. Radcliffe-Brown expressed himself on totemism, in 1929, in terms as negative as those of Boas; but he nevertheless continued to lay stress on the Australian facts, proposing distinctions which are practically the same as those adopted by Elkin. But while Radcliffe-Brown used these distinctions in order to explode the notion of totemism, Elkin proceeds in another fashion. From the diversity of Australian forms of totemism, he does not conclude—as did Tylor, Boas, and Radcliffe-Brown himself—that the notion of totemism is inconsistent and that a careful re-examination of the facts leads to its dissolution. He confines himself to denying their unity, as if he thought it possible to preserve the reality of totemism on condition that it be reduced to a multiplicity of heterogeneous forms. For him, there is no longer totemism but totemisms, each of which exists as an irreducible entity. Instead of contributing to the destruction of the Hydra (and in a field where this would have been decisive, because of the part played by Australian facts in the elaboration of theories of totemism), Elkin chops it up and comes to terms with the pieces. But it is the very idea of totemism that is illusory, not just its unity. In other words, Elkin thinks he can *reify* totemism on the single condition of *atomizing* it. To parody the Cartesian formula, one might say that he divides the difficulty *under pretext* of being able to resolve it.

The attempt would be harmless, and might simply be classed as the forty-second, forty-third, or forty-fourth theory of totemism, if only, unlike the majority of his predecessors, Elkin were not a great ethnographer. In such a case there is the risk that the theory may rebound on empirical reality and disintegrate it under the shock. And this is what has happened: the homogeneity and regularity of the Australian facts (which accounts for their pre-eminent place in anthropological speculation) could be preserved, but on condition of renouncing totemism as a synthetic mode of their reality; or else, totemism could be retained as a real series—even in its plurality—but with the risk that the facts themselves should be infected by this pluralism. Instead of letting theory go in order to respect the facts better, Elkin dissociates the facts so that the theory shall be saved. But in order to preserve the reality of totemism at any price, he risks reducing Australian ethnography to a collection of heterogeneous facts between which it becomes impossible to re-establish any continuity.

In what condition, then, had Elkin found Australian ethnography? With scarcely any doubt, it had nearly succumbed to the ravages of a spirit of systematization. It was all too tempting, as we have observed, to consider only the forms which seemed best organized, to arrange these in order of increasing complexity, and then resolutely to underestimate those aspects which—like Aranda totemism—were difficult to fit in.

But, faced with a situation of this type, there are two ways of proceeding: either to throw out the baby with the bath water, i.e., to give up all hope of reaching a systematic interpretation rather than start all over again, or to be inspired by sufficient confidence in the outlines of order already discerned to broaden one's perspective, seeking a more general point of view which will permit the integration of forms whose regularity has already been established but whose resistance to systematization may perhaps be explained, not by intrinsic characteristics, but by the fact that they have been ill defined, incompletely analyzed, or viewed in too narrow a fashion.

The problem is presented, and in precisely these terms, in connection with rules of marriage and kinship systems, and in another work we have set ourselves the formulation of a general interpretation which takes account simultaneously of systems which had already been analyzed and of others still regarded as irregular or aberrant. We have tried to show that it is possible to make a coherent interpretation of the generality of facts of this type *on condition that we change the generally held conception of rules of marriage and kinship systems.*

Now in the case of totemism, Elkin prefers not to question the idea (with the reservation that the alleged sociological "species" be replaced with varieties which are irreducible and, by this very fact, themselves become species), and to resign himself to the fragmentation of the phenomena. It seems to us, on the contrary (though this is not the place to attempt a demonstration),* that it would have been better, by applying the procedure indicated in the preceding paragraph, to see if it might not be possible to widen the field of interpretation and then to add supplementary dimensions, in the hope of setting up an overall system, but bringing together this time both social *and religious* phenomena, even if the synthetic notion of totemism has to give way before this treatment.

VI

Let us return to the arithmetic progression of classes, since everything starts from there. As we have recalled, many authors have interpreted this as a genetic series. In fact, things are not so simple, for moieties do not "transform" themselves into sections, nor sections into sub-sections. The logical scheme does not consist of three stages, which one might suppose to follow each other in the order 2-4-8, but is instead of the type:

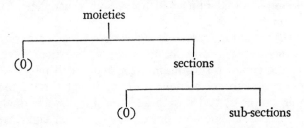

In other words, a system may have only moieties, or sections, or sub-sections, or it may be composed, furthermore, of any two of these forms to the exclusion of the third, as Elkin has shown. But must it therefore be concluded that the *raison d'être* of these

* Cf. *La Pensée Sauvage*, ch. III.

modes of grouping cannot be found at the sociological level, but must be sought on that of religion?

Let us first consider the most simple case. The theory of dual organizations has long suffered from a major confusion between moiety systems, given empirically and observable in an institutionalized state, and dualism as a scheme which is always implied in moiety systems but which is also to be discerned elsewhere, in forms of varying degrees of objectification, and which may even be universal. Now this dualistic scheme underlies, not only moiety systems, but section-systems and sub-section systems as well; and it is displayed by the fact that sections and subsections are always multiples of 2. It is therefore a false problem to ask whether moiety systems necessarily precede in time forms which are more complex. They may do so where the scheme is already institutionalized; but the dualistic scheme may also assume directly, on the institutional level, a more developed form. It is thus conceivable that, according to circumstance, the simple form may be born by reabsorption from the complex form, or that it may indeed precede it in time. The former hypothesis was favored by Boas,[3] but it is certainly not the only possible means of formation, for we have ourselves seen a dual organization form under our eyes, among the Nambikwara of central Brazil, not by the reduction of more numerous groups but by the combination of two simple social units which previously had been isolated from each other.

Dualism cannot therefore be conceived of as a primitive social structure, or as anterior to others. Schematically, at least, it forms the common substratum of systems with moieties, with sections, and with sub-sections. Still, it is not certain that the reasoning can be extended to these latter, for—unlike dualism—a quadripartite scheme does not exist, nor one of eight parts, in the thought of the Australian aborigines, *independently of concrete institutions* which display structures of this type. From the whole of Australia, there is only one case reported in which the division into four sections (each designated in this instance by the name of a different species of sparrowhawk) might have derived from an exhaustive and systematic quadripartition. Moreover, if the divisions into sections and sub-sections were independent of their social functions, they ought to be found in any number. To say that sections are always four, and sub-sections eight, would be tautological, since their number is part of their definition; but it is significant that the anthropologists of Australia have not found it necessary to coin other terms in order to characterize systems of direct exchange. Admittedly, six-section systems have been reported from Australia; but they are actually societies with four sections which have been led by frequent intermarriage to designate two of their respective sections by the same name:

SOCIETY I			SOCIETY II	
a	$(c$	=	$e)$	g
b	$(d$	=	$f)$	h

It is true that Radcliffe-Brown has shown that in the regulation of marriage the Kariera concern themselves less with membership of an appropriate section than with degree of relationship. And among the Wulamba (previously called Murngin) of Arnhem Land, the sub-sections play no real part in the regulation of marriage, since this is contracted with the matrilateral female cross-cousin, which would accord better with a system of four sections. More generally, preferred or prescribed spouses, though they belong normally to a given class (section or sub-section), are not the only ones to occupy it. Hence the idea that the regulation of marriage is not the only, or even perhaps the main, function of the sections: according to a number of authors, such as Elkin, they form instead a sort of short-hand method for classing individuals, during inter-tribal ceremonies, into categories of relatives corresponding to the requirements of the ritual.

They may, of course, fulfill this function in the fashion of a simplified code which is thus more easy to use when there is question concerning equivalences between several dialects or languages. Because it is simplified in relation to the kinship systems proper to each of the groups, this code necessarily neglects the differences. Yet if it is to satisfy its function it cannot contradict the more complex codes either. To recognize that each tribe possesses two codes to express its social structure—kinship system and rules of marriage on the one hand, organization into sections or sub-sections on the other—does not at all entail, and even excludes, that the codes shall by nature be destined to transmit different messages. The message remains the same; only the circumstances and the recipients differ: "The Murngin subsections are based on a system of marriage and descent and they are essentially a kinship structure. They generalize on the larger kinship structure with its great number of relatives by placing a group of these relatives together and calling them by one term. By this regrouping process, all the kinship terms are reduced to eight, since the subsection system has eight divisions." [4]

The method is particularly useful during inter-tribal gatherings: "Some of the people come from hundreds of miles for these great ceremonies . . . and their *kinship* terminology is utterly different. Since the section terms are practically the same and only eight in number, it is comparatively easy to discover one's subsection relationship to an utter stranger." [5] But, as we have shown elsewhere, it would be a mistake to conclude that: ". . . Contrary to the opinion of the older writers, the subsection and section system does not regulate marriage . . . because the relationship of a woman and man finally determines what persons they marry. [A Murngin man] can marry a woman of B^1 or B^2 if he is an A^1 or A^2." [6]

Certainly; but (1) he may not marry anyone else, and the system thus expresses, in its own way, a regulation of marriage at the level of four sections, if not of the sub-sections; (2) even at the sub-section level, congruence is re-established between class and kinship relation, given that the two types of marriage are practiced alternately; (3) the "opinion of the older writers" was based on the examination of groups which, while they may not themselves have thought of the eight-section system with all its sociological implications, had at least perfectly assimilated it. This is not the case with the Murngin, who cannot be placed on the same level.

There is therefore no reason whatever, we believe, to go back on the traditional conception of marriage classes.

A four-section system can be explained only as the sociological process of integration of a double dualism (without the one being necessarily historically anterior to the other), and the eight-section system as a reduplication of the same process. For, even though there is no necessity that four-section systems should previously have been moiety systems, it nevertheless seems reasonable to postulate a genetic relation between eight-section and four-section systems; firstly because if this were not the case we ought to be able to observe systems endowed with any number of sub-divisions whatever; and secondly because while the double duality is still a duality, a triple duality introduces a new principle. This is revealed in the Ambrym-Pentecost type of six-section system. But these systems precisely are lacking in Australia,* where eight-section systems can therefore only be the result of an operation of the type: 2×4.

How to interpret, then, the cases adduced by Elkin in which the sub-sections seem to be purely totemic, without any bearing on the regulation of marriage? To begin with, the use to which he puts these examples is not absolutely convincing. Let us confine ourselves to the case of the Murngin. The sub-section system is so little foreign to the regulation of marriage that it has been manipulated, in an ingenious and complicated way, to the sole end of re-establishing a correspondence: in constituting the sub-sections, the natives changed their mechanism (by the introduction of an optional rule of marriage applying to one marriage in two) in such a way as to eliminate the effect of the division into sub-sections on the marital exchanges. The only conclusion that may be drawn from this example is that in having recourse to the sub-sections the Murngin were not trying to apply a method of securing social integration better than that which they had previously, or one based on different principles. While retaining

* The contrary has been maintained (Lane, 1960), but although a system of the type called Karadjeri may theoretically function with only three lines, nothing in the reported facts suggests an actual tripartition, since Elkin has himself established the existence of a fourth line (Elkin, 1954, reprinting of 1961, pp. 77-79).

a traditional structure, they dressed it up, as one might say, by disguising it in externals borrowed from neighboring peoples, being motivated by the admiration which is apparently inspired in Australian aborigines by very complicated social institutions.

Other examples of such borrowing are known. Formerly the Murinbata had only patrilineal moieties. The sub-sections are a recent introduction, imported by some exceptionally intelligent natives who were great travelers and had sought instruction in foreign camps, where they had perfectly mastered the mechanism of the sub-sections. Even when they are not understood, these rules enjoy a considerable prestige, though here and there reactionaries protest against them. Without any doubt, the sub-section system exerts an irresistible attraction on these tribes. However, because of the patrilineal character of the previous system, the sub-sections have been clumsily assigned, and the result is a large number of marriages which from a formal point of view are irregular, although relations of kinship are still respected.[7]

Sometimes, too, a system imposed from without remains incomprehensible. T. G. H. Strehlow relates the story of two southern Aranda who were classed by neighbors who had come from the north into different sub-sections, even though they themselves had always called each other brother:

The two old Southern men had been put into separate classes by these newcomers, since one of them had married a wife who came from an eight-class group; and the marriage had now been "legalized" according to the ideas of the strangers. They finished their explanation with some very scathing remarks about the Northern Aranda who had had the presumption of attempting to force their own system upon old Southern territory, where men had lived orderly lives under the four-section system as far back as memory and tradition could reach.

"The old four-class system is the better of the two for us Southerners; we cannot understand the eight-class system. It is mad and purposeless, and only fit for such crazy men as the Northern Aranda are; *we* did not inherit such stupid traditions from *our* fathers."[8]

Let us suppose, therefore, that each time the sections or sub-sections were invented, copied, or intelligently borrowed, their function was firstly sociological, i.e., they served—and still serve —to encode, in a relatively simple form applicable beyond the tribal borders, the kinship system and that of marital exchange. But once these institutions were given, they began to lead an independent existence, as objects of curiosity or aesthetic admiration, and also as symbols, by their very complication, of a higher type of culture. They must often have been adopted, for their own sake, by neighboring peoples who understood their function imperfectly. In such cases, they have been only approximately adjusted to pre-existing social rules, or even not at all. Their mode of existence remains ideological, and the natives "play" at sections or sub-sections, or they submit to them without really knowing how to use them. In other words, and contrary to Elkin's belief, *it is not because they are totemic that such systems must be regarded as irregular; it is because they are irregular that they can only be totemic,* totemism—instead of the social organization —then supplying, by reason of its speculative and gratuitous character, the only level on which it is possible for them to function. Besides, the term "irregular" has not the same meaning in both cases. Elkin adduces these examples as an implicit condemnation of all effort at systematic typology, which he tends to replace by a simple inventory, or empirical description, of heterogeneous modalities. But for us the term "irregular" does not contradict the existence of regular forms; it is applied only to pathological forms, which are less frequent than some like to think, and the reality of which—supposing this to be clearly established —could not be placed on a par with that of normal forms. As Marx said, the eruption on the skin is not as positive as the skin from which it springs.

Behind the empirical categories of Elkin, moreover, can one not divine the outline of a system? He opposes the totemism of matrilineal clans to that of patrilineal clans, and with good reason. In the former case, the totem is "flesh," in the latter it is "dream"; organic and material in one case, therefore, spiritual and incorporeal in the other. Moreover, matrilineal totemism attests the diachronic and biological continuity of the clan, it is the flesh and blood perpetuated from generation to generation by the women of the lineage; while patrilineal totemism expresses "the local solidarity of the horde," i.e., an external link, no longer an internal one, territorial and no longer biological, which synchronically—no longer diachronically—unites the members of the clan.

All this is true, but must we therefore conclude that we are dealing with different sociological "species"? This is so little certain that the opposition may even be reversed: matrilineal totemism also has a synchronic function, which is to express, in each patrilocal territory where spouses come to reside from different clans, the differential structure of the tribal group. Patrilineal totemism, in its turn, has a diachronic function: it expresses the temporal continuity of the horde, commemorating periodically, through the ministrations of cult groups, the installation of mythical ancestors in a certain territory.

Far from appearing heterogeneous, therefore, the two forms seen rather to be in a relationship of complementarity. There is a passage from one to the other by way of transformations. Although the means are different, they both establish a connection between the material and the spiritual world, between diachronic and synchronic, structure and event. These are two different but correlative ways, two possible ways among others, of displaying parallel attributes of nature and society.

Elkin senses this so well that after cutting up totemism into distinct entities, he strives to return some unity to them. All types of totemism, he concludes, fulfill a double function, i.e., to express on the one hand the kinship and cooperation of man with nature, and on the other the continuity between past and present. But the formula is so vague and general that one no longer understands why this temporal continuity should entail that the first ancestors had to have animal shape, nor why the solidarity of the social group had necessarily to be affirmed in the form of a plurality of cults. It is not only totemism but all philosophy and religion, of whatever kind, that presents the features by which Elkin attempts to define the first: "a philosophy which . . . provides that faith, hope, and courage in the face of his daily needs, which man must have if he is to persevere and persist, both as an individual and as a social being." [9]

Were so many observations and so many enquiries necessary to end up with such a conclusion? There is no link to be seen between Elkin's rich and penetrating enquiries and this summary synthesis. The gap between the two levels recalls irresistibly that with which, in the eighteenth century, certain people criticized Grétry's harmony, saying that between his high notes and his low you could drive a carriage.

THREE

Functionalist Theories of Totemism

I

We have seen how Elkin tries to save totemism: by splitting his forces to let the American offensive pass through while he regroups his troops on both flanks, one resting on a finer analysis, the other on a blunter synthesis, than those of his predecessors. But this strategy really reflects the main influences to which he has been subjected, and which drag him in opposite directions: from Radcliffe-Brown he received a careful method of observation and the taste for classification, while the example of Malinowski inclined him toward hasty generalizations and eclectic solutions. Elkin's analyses are inspired by the lessons of Radcliffe-Brown; his attempt at synthesis joins with that of Malinowski.

Malinowski accepts, in fact, the reality of totemism. Nevertheless, his answer to American criticisms does not consist, as does that of Elkin, in re-establishing totemism on the facts, at the price of cutting it up into distinct entities, but in first transcending the level of observation in order to grasp totemism intuitively in its regained unity and simplicity. To this end, Malinowski adopts a perspective which is more biological and psychological than anthropological. The interpretation he offers is naturalistic, utilitarian, and affective.

For him, the alleged totemic problem boils down to three questions which are easy to answer when they are taken separately. First, why is totemism concerned with animals and plants? It is because these supply man with his food, and because the need for food takes first place in the consciousness of the primitive, arousing intense and varied emotions. There is nothing surprising in the fact that a certain number of animal and vegetable species, which form the staple diet of the tribe, should become a major focus of interest for its members:

> The road from the wilderness to the savage's belly and conse-
> quently to his mind is very short, and for him the world is an in-
> discriminate background against which there stand out the useful,
> primarily the edible, species of animals and plants.[1]

It may be asked, secondly, what is the basis of the belief in an affinity between man and animals and plants, the rites of multiplication, food tabus, and sacramental forms of consumption. The affinity between man and animal is easily verifiable: like man, the animal moves, emits sounds, expresses its emotions, has a body and a face. What is more, its powers seem superior to those of man: the bird flies, the fish swims, reptiles shed their skin. The animal occupies an intermediary position between man and nature, and inspires in the former a mixture of feelings: admiration or fear, and lust for food, which are the ingredients of totemism. Inanimate objects—plants, natural phenomena, or manufactured objects—come into the picture only as a "secondary formation . . . which has nothing to do with the substance of totemism."

As for cults, they correspond to the desire to control the species, whether this is edible, useful, or dangerous, and the belief in such a power brings with it the idea of a community of life: man and animal have to participate in the same nature in order that the former shall be able to act on the latter. This results in "obvious restrictions" such as the prohibition on killing or eating the animal, as well as the correlative claim to the power, vested in man, to produce its multiplication.

The last question concerns the concomitance, in totemism, of a social and a religious aspect, for so far only the former has been taken into consideration. But this is because all ritual tends toward magic, and all magic leads to individual or familial specialization:

> In totemism the magical multiplication of each species would
> naturally become the duty and privilege of a specialist, assisted by
> his family.[2]

As the family itself tends to change into a clan, the attribution of a different totem to each clan poses no problem.

In this way, totemism is seen as perfectly natural:

> Totemism appears thus as a blessing bestowed by religion on primitive man's efforts in dealing with his useful surroundings, upon his "struggle for existence." [3]

The problem is therefore doubly turned upside down: totemism is no longer a cultural phenomenon but "the result of natural conditions." By its origin and its manifestations it belongs to biology and psychology, not to anthropology. The question is no longer to know why totemism exists where it exists, and in different forms the observation, description, and analysis of which offer no more than a secondary interest. The only question which presents itself—but does it?—is to understand why it does not exist everywhere. . . .

Let us be careful not to imagine that totemism has vanished like a cloud at the tap of the fairy wand—slight enough, in both senses of the word—of Malinowski. The problem has been simply turned round. It is only anthropology, with all its conquests, its knowledge, and its methods, that might well have disappeared from the scene.

II

Toward the end of his life, Radcliffe-Brown was to contribute decisively to the solution of the problem of totemism by his success in isolating and disclosing the real problems which lay hidden behind the phantasmagoria of the theorists. We shall call this his second theory. But it is essential to begin by examining the first, the development of which, though it was more analytical and rigorous in principle than Malinowski's, nevertheless led to very similar conclusions.

While Radcliffe-Brown would probably not willingly have admitted it, his point of departure merges with that of Boas. Like the latter, he asks himself whether "the term totemism, taken in its technical sense, has not outlived its use." Like Boas, and almost in the same words, he announces his project as being to reduce the alleged totemism to a particular case of relations between man and natural species, such as these are formulated in myths and ritual.

The idea of totemism is composed of elements taken from different institutions. In Australia alone it is necessary to distinguish many kinds of totemism: sexual, local, individual; by moiety, section, sub-section, clan (patrilineal, matrilineal), horde, etc.: "The only thing that these totemic systems have in common is the general tendency to characterise the segments into which society is divided by an association between each segment and some natural species or some portion of nature. This association may take any one of a number of forms." [4]

So far, attempts have usually been made to ascertain the origin of each form. But since we know nothing, or practically nothing, about the past of primitive societies, the undertaking remains conjectural and speculative.

Radcliffe-Brown wishes to substitute for such historical investigations an inductive method inspired by the natural sciences. Behind the empirical complexity, we have therefore to seek certain simple principles:

Can we show that totemism is a special form of a phenomenon which is universal in human society and is therefore present in different forms in all cultures? [5]

Durkheim was the first to frame the question in these terms. Radcliffe-Brown, while paying him respect, rejects his argument as proceeding from an incomplete analysis of the notion of the sacred. To say that the totem is sacred comes down to stating that there is a ritual relation between man and his totem, it being understood that by "ritual relation" is meant a collection of attitudes and obligatory ways of behaving. Consequently, the notion of the sacred does not supply an explanation; it merely refers the issue to the general problem of ritual relations.

In order that social order shall be maintained (and if it were not there would be no problem, since the society considered would disappear or would change into a different society), it is necessary to assure the permanence and solidarity of the clans which compose the society. This permanence and solidarity can be based only on individual sentiments, and these, in order to be expressed efficaciously, demand a collective expression which has to be fixed on concrete objects:

individual sentiments of attachment
↓
ritualized collective conduct
↓
object representing the group

This explains the place assigned to symbols such as flags, kings, presidents, etc., in contemporary societies.

But why does totemism call on animals or plants? Durkheim gives a contingent explanation of this phenomenon: the permanence and continuity of the clan require only an emblem, which may be—and which must be at first—an arbitrary sign, so simple that any society whatever, even when it lacks all means of artistic expression, may conceive the idea of it. If it is later "recognized" that these signs represent animals or plants, this is because animals and plants are present, accessible, and easy to signify. For Durkheim, consequently, the place accorded to animals and plants in totemism constitutes a sort of delayed consequence. It was natural that it should be produced, but it has nothing essential about it. Radcliffe-Brown maintains, to the contrary, that the ritualization of relations between man and animal supplies a wider and more general frame than totemism, and within which totemism must have developed. This ritual attitude is attested among peoples without totemism, such as the Eskimo, and there are other such examples, equally independent of totemism, since the Andaman Islanders observe a ritual conduct toward the turtles which occupy an important place in their means of subsistence, and so do the Californian Indians toward the salmon, and all the peoples of the Arctic toward the bear. These modes of behavior, in fact, are found universally in hunting societies.

Matters would remain at this point if there were no social

segmentation. But once this is produced, ritual and religious segmentation follows automatically. Thus in Roman Catholicism the worship of saints developed together with the organization of parishes and religious individualization. The same tendency is present in outline at least among the Eskimo, with their division into "winter people" and "summer people," and their corresponding ritual dichotomy.

On the dual condition of conceding—what observation suggests everywhere and at all periods—that natural interests give rise to ritual conduct, and that ritual segmentation follows social, the problem of totemism disappears and gives way to a different problem, but one which has the advantage of being far more general, viz.: "Why do the majority of what are called primitive peoples adopt in their custom and myth a ritual attitude towards animals and other species?" [6]

The examples above, Radcliffe-Brown thinks, have supplied the answer: it is a universally attested fact that every thing and every event which exercises an important influence on the material or spiritual well-being of society tends to become an object of a ritual attitude. If totemism chose natural species to serve as social emblems for segments of the society, this is quite simply because these species were already objects of ritual attitudes before totemism.

Radcliffe-Brown thus reverses the Durkheimian interpretation, according to which the totems are objects of ritual attitudes ("sacred" in Durkheim's terminology) because they were first called upon to serve as social emblems. For Radcliffe-Brown, nature is incorporated in the social order rather than being subordinated to it. Indeed, at this stage in the evolution of his thought, Radcliffe-Brown "naturalizes," as it were, the thought of Durkheim. He could hardly accept that a method ostensibly taken from the natural sciences might lead to the paradoxical result of establishing the social on a separate plane. To say that anthropology is amenable to the method of natural science is, for him, to maintain that anthropology is a natural science. It is not enough, therefore, to observe, describe, and classify as the natural sciences do, though on a different level; the object of observation must itself belong to nature, even if humbly. The final interpretation of totemism ascribes primacy to social segmentation over ritual and religious segmentation, each remaining, by the same token, a function of "natural" interests. According to Radcliffe-Brown's first theory, as for Malinowski, an animal only becomes "totemic" because it is first "good to eat."

III

However, an incomparable fieldworker such as Malinowski knew better than any that you cannot get to the bottom of a concrete problem by means of generalities. When he studies totemism, not in general but in the particular form which it assumes in the Trobriands, biological, psychological, and moral considerations abandon the field to ethnography, and even to history.

Near the village of Laba'i there is a hole called Obukula from which the four clans which compose Trobriand society are believed to have emerged from the depths of the earth. The first to come out was the iguana, the animal of Lukulabuta clan; then the dog, of Lukuba clan, which then took first place; then the pig, representative of Malasi clan, which is the principal clan at present; and finally the totem of Lukwasisiga, which was the crocodile, snake, or opossum, according to different versions of the myth. The dog and the pig began to wander here and there; the dog found a fruit on the ground, from the *noku* tree, sniffed it, and ate it. Then the pig said to the dog: "You have eaten *noku,* you have eaten filth, you are of low birth. I shall be the chief." Thenceforth the office of chief belongs to the highest lineage of Malasi clan. The fruit of the *noku,* which is gathered only in time of scarcity, is actually regarded as an inferior kind of food.[7]

On the admission of Malinowski himself, these animals are far from being of equal importance in the native culture. To say, as he does, that the unimportance of the first one—the iguana —and of the later arrivals—crocodile, snake, or opossum—is explained by the inferior rank assigned to the corresponding clans, is in contradiction with his general theory of totemism, since this is a cultural and not a natural explanation, sociological and no longer biological. To account for the hierarchy of the clans, moreover, Malinowski has to construct a hypothesis according to which two clans are descended from invaders who came by sea, while the two others are autochthonous. Besides the fact that this hypothesis is historical, and thus not universal (contrary to the general theory, which claims to be universal), it suggests that the dog and the pig might figure in the myth as "cultural" animals, and the others as "natural" in that they are more closely associated with the earth, water, or the forest. But if one were to take this path, or a similar one, it would be necessary first to turn to Melanesian ethno-zoology (i.e., the positive knowledge which the natives of this part of the world possess concerning animals, the technical and ritual uses to which they put them, and the beliefs they hold about them), and not to utilitarian prejudices resting on no particular empirical foundation. Moreover, it is clear that relationships such as we have just mentioned by way of example are *conceived,* not *experienced.* In formulating them, the mind allows itself to be guided by a theoretical rather than by a practical aim.

In the second place, a search for utility at any price runs up against those innumerable cases in which the totemic animals or plants have no discernible use from the point of view of the native culture. To adhere strictly to principle, it is necessary to manipulate the notion of interest, giving it an appropriate meaning on each occasion, in such a way that the empirical exigency postulated in the beginning is progressively changed into verbal juggling, *petitio principii,* or tautology. Malinowski himself is unable to hold to the axiom (though it is the basis of his system) reducing the totemic species to useful and, above all, edible species: immediately, he has to propose other motives, such as admiration or fear. But why then does one find in Australia such odd totems as laughing, various illnesses, vomiting, and a corpse?

An obstinate taste for utilitarian interpretations sometimes leads to a strange dialectic. Thus Ursula McConnel maintains that the totems of the Wikmunkan (on the Gulf of Carpentaria, in northern Australia) reflect economic interests: the totems of the coastal tribes are the dugong, sea turtle, various sharks, crabs, oysters, and other mollusks, as well as thunder, "which announces the season of the north wind," high tide, "which brings food," and a little bird which is "believed to protect fishing operations." The peoples of the interior have totems which are also related to their environment: bush rat, wallaby, young grass "that the animals feed on," arrowroot, yam, etc.

It is more difficult to explain the affection for the shooting star—another totem—"which announces the death of a relative." But, the author continues, this is because in addition to their positive function, or instead of it, "totems may represent dangerous and disagreeable objects, such as 'crocodiles' and 'flies' [elsewhere, mosquitoes as well] which possess a negative social interest in that they cannot be ignored but may be increased for the discomfort of enemies and strangers." [8] In this respect, it would be difficult to find anything which, in one way or another, positively or negatively (or even because of its lack of significance?), might not be said to offer an interest, and the utilitarian and naturalist theory would thus be reduced to a series of propositions empty of any content.

Moreover, Spencer and Gillen long ago suggested a much more satisfying explanation of the inclusion among the totems of species which a naive utilitarianism would regard simply as harmful: "Flies and mosquitos . . . are such pests that, at first sight, it is not easy to understand why ceremonies to increase their number should be performed. . . . However, it must be remembered that flies and mosquitoes, though themselves intensely objectionable, are very intimately associated with what the native above all things desires to see at certain times of the year, and that is a heavy rainfall." [9] Which is to say—and the formula might be extended to the entire field of totemism—that flies and mosquitoes are not perceived as *stimuli*, but are conceived as *signs*.

In the work which we examined in the preceding chapter, Firth still seems to tend toward utilitarian explanations. The yam, taro, coconut, and breadfruit are the staple foods of Tikopia, and, as such, are regarded as being infinitely precious. However, when we wish to understand why edible fish are excluded from the totemic system, this type of explanation has to be qualified: before the activity of fishing, fish constitute a vague and undifferentiated entity; they are not present and observable, as are food plants in the gardens and orchards. So fishing rituals are not divided among the clans; the latter perform them in common around the sacred canoes with the aid of which men secure fish. When food plants are concerned, society is interested in their increase; in the case of fish, it is interested in catching them.[10]

The theory is ingenious, but even if it is accepted it still shows that the relation between man and his needs is mediated by culture and cannot be conceived of simply in terms of nature. As Firth himself remarks, "As far as the majority of animal totem species is concerned the economic interest in them is not of a pronounced type." [11] Even as far as vegetable foods are concerned, another work by Firth suggests that matters are more complex than a utilitarian interpretation allows for. The idea of economic interest includes many aspects which should be distinguished, and which do not always coincide with each other, nor each of them with social and religious behavior. Food plants may thus be ranked in a hierarchical order of decreasing importance, according to their place in subsistence (I), the labor necessary to grow them (II), the complexity of the ritual intended to make them flourish (III), the complexity of the harvest rites (IV), and finally the religious importance of the clans which control the main kinds (V), viz., Kafika (yam), Taumako (taro), Tafua (coconut), Fangarere (breadfruit). The information recorded by Firth[12] is summed up in the following table:

(I)	(II)	(III)	(IV)	(V)
taro	taro	yam	yam	Kafika
breadfruit	yam	taro	taro	Taumako
coconut	*pulaka* (*Alocasia sp.*)	coconut	breadfruit	Fangarere
banana	coconut	banana	sago	Fusi (house of Tafua)
pulaka	banana	breadfruit	coconut	Tafua
sago	breadfruit	sago	banana	(none)
yam	sago	*pulaka*	*pulaka*	(none)

The table does not correspond with the totemic system, since the number of plants in it is greater; the yam, which is controlled by the highest clan, and the ritual of which, both for its cultivation and for its harvest, is also the most complex, occupies the last place in importance as food and the second in labor demanded. The "non-totemic" banana tree and sago palm are objects of more important ritual, both to raise them and to gather their fruits, than are the breadfruit tree and the coconut palm, both of which are nevertheless "totemic," and so on.

IV

It is not very likely that Radcliffe-Brown had a clear idea of the evolution of his own thought over the last thirty years of his life, for even his latest writings keep closely to the line that he took in his older works. Moreover, the evolution did not take place progressively: one might say that two tendencies were always co-present in him, and that according to occasion sometimes the one and sometimes the other was expressed. As he grew older, each tendency became more precise and refined, making the opposition between them more obvious, but it is impossible to say which of the two would finally have prevailed.

We should therefore not be too surprised that, exactly ten years after he had formulated his first theory of totemism, Radcliffe-Brown should have opposed Malinowski with regard to magic and that his ideas about the phenomenon, though very close to those of the other, should have been as far removed as possible from his own earlier ones. Malinowski, in a more consistent fashion, had treated the problem of magic in the same way as that of totemism, i.e., by reference to general psychological considerations. All magical rites and practices were reduced to a means for man to abolish or diminish the anxiety which he felt in undertakings of uncertain outcome. Magic thus has, according to him, a practical and affective end.

It should be noted immediately that the connection postulated by Malinowski between magic and risk is not at all obvious. Every undertaking involves some risk, if only that of failing, or that the result shall not plainly match the hopes of the actor. Yet in all societies magic occupies a clearly delimited zone which includes certain undertakings and leaves others outside. To maintain that the former are precisely those which the society regards as uncertain would be to beg the question, for there is no objective criterion for deciding which undertakings, independently of the fact that some of them are accompanied by rituals, are held by human societies to be more or less risky. Societies are known in which types of activity which involve certain danger have no connection with magic. This is the case, for example, among the Ngindo, a small Bantu tribe, living at a very low technical and economic level, who lead a precarious existence in the forests of southern Tanganyika, and among whom apiculture plays an important part: "Seeing that bee-keeping is such a risky business, involving nocturnal wandering in hostile forest, and encounters with hostile bees at dizzy heights, its dearth of attendant ritual might seem astounding. But it has been pointed out to me that danger does not necessarily evoke ritual. Some hunting tribes are known to go after big game without overmuch formality. Ritual impinges very little on the Ngindo daily subsistence routine." [13]

The empirical relationship postulated by Malinowski is thus not verified. And in any case, as Radcliffe-Brown remarks, the argument proposed (which merely recapitulates, moreover, that of Loisy) would be just as plausible if it were turned round the other way, producing an exactly opposite thesis:

. . . namely, that if it were not for the existence of the rite and the beliefs associated with it the individual would feel no anxiety, and that the psychological effect of the rite is to create in him a sense of insecurity or danger. It seems very unlikely that an Andaman Islander would think it is dangerous to eat dugong or pork or turtle meat if it were not for the existence of a specific body of ritual the ostensible purpose of which is to protect him from these dangers . . . Thus, while one anthropological theory is that magic and religion give men confidence, comfort and a sense of security, it could equally well be argued that they give men fears and anxieties from which they would otherwise be free. . . .[14]

Thus it is certainly not because men feel anxiety in certain situations that they turn to magic, but it is because they have recourse to magic that these situations engender anxiety in them. Now this argument also applies to Radcliffe-Brown's first theory of totemism, since this affirms that men adopt a ritual attitude toward animal and vegetable species which arouse their interest (which should be understood as: their spontaneous interest). Could it not just as well be maintained that (as the bizarre nature of the lists of totems suggests) it is rather because of the ritual attitudes which they observe toward certain species that men are led to find an interest in them?

We may certainly imagine that in the beginning of social life, and today still, individuals who were prey to anxiety should have originated, and still originate, compulsive modes of behavior such as are observed among psychopaths; and that a kind of social selection should have operated on this multitude of individual variations in such a way, like natural selection by means of mutations, as to preserve and generalize those that were useful to the perpetuation of the group and the maintenance of order, and to eliminate the others. But this hypothesis, which is difficult to verify for the present, and impossible for the distant past, would add nothing to the simple statement that rites are born and disappear irregularly.

Before a recourse to anxiety could supply even the outlines of an explanation, we should have to know what anxiety actually is, and then what relations exist between, on the one hand, a confused and disordered emotion, and, on the other, acts marked by the most rigorous precision and which are divided into a number of distinct categories. By what mechanism might the former give rise to the latter? Anxiety is not a cause: it is the way in which man perceives, subjectively and obscurely, an internal disorder such that he does not even know whether it is physical or mental. If an intelligible connection exists, it has to be sought between articulated modes of behavior and structures of disorder of which the theory has yet to be worked out, not between behavior and the reflection of unknown phenomena on the screen of sensation.

Psycho-analytical theory, which Malinowski implicitly makes use of, sets itself the task of teaching us that the behavior of disturbed persons is symbolic, and that its interpretation calls for a grammar, i.e., a code which, like all codes, is by its very nature extra-individual. This behavior may be accompanied by anxiety, but it is not anxiety that produces it. The fundamental error in Malinowski's thesis is that it takes for a cause what, in the most favorable circumstances, is only a consequence or a concomitant.

As affectivity is the most obscure side of man, there has been the constant temptation to resort to it, forgetting that what is refractory to explanation is *ipso facto* unsuitable for use in explanation. A datum is not primary because it is incomprehensible: this characteristic indicates solely that an explanation, if it exists, must be sought on another level. Otherwise, we shall be satisfied to attach another label to the problem, thus believing it to have been solved.

The first stage of Radcliffe-Brown's thought is sufficient to demonstrate that this illusion has vitiated reflections on totemism. It is this, also, which ruins Freud's attempt in *Totem and Taboo*. It is well known that Kroeber changed his mind somewhat about this work twenty years after condemning it for its inexactitudes and unscientific method. In 1939, however, he accused himself of injustice: had he not used a sledge-hammer to crush a butterfly? If Freud gave up the idea, as he seemed to have done, that the act of parricide was a historical event, it could be viewed as the symbolic expression of a recurrent virtuality, a generic and non-temporal model of psychological attitudes entailed by repetitive phenomena or institutions such as totemism and tabus.[15]

But this is not the real question. Contrary to what Freud maintained, social constraints, whether positive or negative, cannot be explained, either in their origin or in their persistence, as the effects of impulses or emotions which appear again and again, with the same characteristics and during the course of centuries and millennia, in different individuals. For if the recurrence of the sentiments explained the persistence of customs, the origin of the customs ought to coincide with the origin of the appearance of the sentiments, and Freud's thesis would be unchanged even if the parricidal impulse corresponded to a typical situation instead of to a historical event.*

We do not know, and never shall know, anything about the first origin of beliefs and customs the roots of which plunge into a distant past; but, as far as the present is concerned, it is certain that social behavior is not produced spontaneously by each individual, under the influence of emotions of the moment. Men do not act, as members of a group, in accordance with what each feels as an individual; each man feels as a function of the way in which he is permitted or obliged to act. Customs are given as external norms before giving rise to internal sentiments, and these non-sentient norms determine the sentiments of individuals as well as the circumstances in which they may, or must, be displayed.

Moreover, if institutions and customs drew their vitality from being continually refreshed and invigorated by individual sentiments, like those in which they originated, they ought to conceal an affective richness, continually replenished, which would be their positive content. We know that this is not the case, and that the constancy which they exhibit usually results from a conventional attitude. To whatever society he belongs, the individual is rarely capable of assigning a cause to this conformity: all he can say is that things have always been like this, and he does what people before him did. This kind of response seems perfectly veracious. Fervor does not emerge in obedience and in behavior, which would necessarily be the case if each individual adopted social beliefs because at a certain time in his life he had experienced them intimately and personally. Emotion is indeed aroused, but when the custom, in itself indifferent, is violated.

It may seem that we are reverting to Durkheim's position, but in the last analysis Durkheim derives social phenomena as well from affectivity. His theory of totemism starts with an urge,

* Unlike Kroeber's, our attitude toward *Totem and Taboo* has hardened rather over the years. Cf. *Les Structures élémentaires de la parenté* (1949), pp. 609-610.

and ends with a recourse to sentiment. As we have already seen, for him the existence of totems results from the recognition of animal or plant effigies in what were previously only non-figurative and arbitrary signs. But why should men have come to symbolize their clan affiliations by signs? Because, says Durkheim, there is an "instinctive tendency" which leads "men of a lower civilisation . . . associated in a common life . . . to paint or incise on the body images which recall this community of existence." [16] This graphic "instinct" is thus the basis of a system which reaches its consummation in an affective theory of the sacred. But Durkheim's theory of the collective origin of the sacred, like those which we have just criticized, rests on a *petitio principii:* it is not present emotions, felt at gatherings and ceremonies, which engender or perpetuate the rites, but ritual activity which arouses the emotions. Far from the religious idea being born of "effervescent social surroundings, and of this very effervescence," [17] they presuppose it.

Actually, impulses and emotions explain nothing: they are always *results,* either of the power of the body or of the impotence of the mind. In both cases they are consequences, never causes. The latter can be sought only in the organism, which is the exclusive concern of biology, or in the intellect, which is the sole way offered to psychology, and to anthropology as well.

FOUR

Toward the Intellect

I

The Tallensi of the northern Gold Coast are divided into patrilineal clans observing distinctive totemic prohibitions. They share this feature with the peoples of the upper Volta, and even with the generality of those of the western Sudan. It is not only a matter of formal resemblance, for the animal species most commonly prohibited are the same over the entire extent of this vast territory, as also are the myths which are invoked to account for the prohibitions.

The objects of the totemic prohibitions of the Tallensi comprise birds such as the canary, turtle-dove, domestic hen; reptiles such as the crocodile, snake, turtle (land and water); certain fish; the large grasshopper; rodents such as the squirrel and hare; ruminants such as the goat and sheep; carnivores such as the cat, dog, and leopard; and, finally, other animals such as the monkey, wild pig, etc.

It is impossible to find any common trait among this variety of creatures. Some play an important part in the economic life and the food-supply of the natives, but the majority are negligible in this respect. Many are prized as delicacies by those who are permitted to eat them; and, on the other hand, some are despised as food. No adult would willingly eat grasshopper, canaries, or small edible snakes, though little children, who eat almost any small animals they can lay their hands on, quite often do so. Several of these animal species are regarded as always potentially dangerous in the magical as well as the physical sense. Such are the crocodile, snakes, the leopard, and other wild carnivores. But many, on the contrary, are entirely innocent both in the magical and the physical sense. Some have a place in the meagre folk-lore of the Tallensi, including such diverse creatures as the monkey, the turtle-dove, and the cat. . . . Incidentally, clans that have the cat as totem show no particular respect towards household cats, nor are household dogs treated differently by people who may and people who may not eat the dog.

The totemic animals of the Tallensi thus comprise neither a zoological nor a utilitarian nor a magical class. All that can be said of them is that they are generally fairly common domestic or wild creatures.[1]

This takes us far from Malinowski. But, above all, Fortes brings out a problem which, since Boas, may be glimpsed behind the illusions created by totemism. To understand beliefs and prohibitions of this order it is not enough to attribute a general function to them, viz., as constituting a simple and concrete procedure which is easily transmissible in the form of habits contracted in childhood, in order to display the complex structure of a society. For yet another question presents itself, and one that is probably fundamental, viz., why the animal symbolism? Above all, and seeing that it has been established, at least negatively, that the choice of certain animals is not explicable from a utilitarian point of view, why such a particular symbolism rather than any other?

Let us take the Tallensi case by stages. There are individual animals, or even sometimes geographically localized species, which are the objects of tabus because they are met with in the neighborhood of shrines dedicated to particular ancestor cults. There is no question of totemism here, in the meaning normally given to the word. "Tabus of the Earth" form an intermediate category between these sacred animals or species and the totems, such as the large reptiles—crocodile, python, tree-lizard or water-lizard—which may not be killed near an Earth shrine. They are "the people of the Earth," in the same sense as men are described as people of such and such a village, and they symbolize the power of the Earth, which may be beneficent or maleficent. The question immediately arises why certain terrestrial creatures have been selected and not others. The python, for example, is particularly sacred in the territory guarded by a certain clan.

Moreover, the animal is more than a simple object of a prohibition; it is an ancestor, and to kill it would be almost as bad as murder. This is not because the Tallensi believe in metempsychosis, but because the ancestors, their human descendants, and the resident animals are all united by a territorial link: "The ancestors . . . are spiritually present in the social life of their descendants in the same way as the sacred animals are present in sacred pools or in the locality with which the group is identified." [2]

Tallensi society is thus comparable to a fabric in which the warp and the woof correspond respectively to localities and to lineages. Intimately connected as they are, these elements nonetheless constitute distinct realities, accompanied by particular sanctions and ritual symbols, within the general framework of the ancestor cult. The Tallensi know that an individual, in his social capacity, combines multiple roles, each of which corresponds to an aspect or a function of the society, and that he is continually confronted by problems of orientation and selection: "Totemic and other ritual symbols are the ideological landmarks that keep an individual on his course." [3] As a member of a large clan, a man is related to common and distant ancestors, symbolized by sacred animals; as member of a lineage, to closer ancestors, symbolized by totems; and lastly, as an individual, he is connected with particular ancestors who reveal his personal fate and who may appear to him through an intermediary such as a domestic animal or certain wild game:

But what is the common psychological theme in these different categories of animals symbolised? The relations between men and their ancestors among the Tallensi are a never-ceasing struggle. Men try to coerce and placate their ancestors by means of sacrifices. But the ancestors are unpredictable. It is their power to injure and their sudden attacks on routine well-being that make men aware of them rather than their beneficent guardianship. It is by their aggressive intervention in human affairs that they control the social order. Do what they will men can never control the ancestors. Like the animals of the bush and the river, they are restless, elusive, ubiquitous, unpredictable, aggressive. The relations of men with animals in the world of common-sense experience are an apt symbolism of the relations of men with their ancestors in the sphere of mystical causation.[4]

Fortes finds in this comparison the explanation for the predominant place assigned to carnivorous animals, those which the Tallensi group together under the term "teeth-bearers," which exist and protect themselves by attacking other animals and sometimes even men: "their symbolic link with the potential aggressiveness of the ancestors is patent." Because of their vitality, these animals are also a convenient symbol for immortality. That this symbolism is always of the same type, viz., animal, is due to the fundamental character of the social and moral code, embodied in the ancestor cult; that different animal symbols should be employed is explained by the fact that this code has different aspects.

In his study of totemism in Polynesia, Firth had already tended toward this type of explanation:

It is a feature of Polynesian totemism that the natural species concerned are generally animals, either land or marine, and that plants, though occasionally included in the list, never predominate. The reason for this preference for animals, it seems to me, lies in the fact that the behavior of the totem is usually held to give an indication as to the actions or intentions of the god concerned. Plants, because of their immobility, are not of much interest from this point of view, and the tendency is then for the more mobile species, endowed with locomotion and versatility of movement, and often with other striking characteristics in the matter of shape, colour, ferocity, or peculiar cries, to be represented in greater measure in the list of media which serve as outlet for the supernatural beings.[5]

These interpretations by Firth and Fortes are much more satisfactory than those of the classical adherents of totemism, or of its first adversaries such as Goldenweiser, because they escape the double danger of recourse either to some arbitrary explanation or to factitious evidence. It is clear that in so-called totemic systems the natural species do not serve as any old names for social units which might just as well have been designated in another way; and it is no less clear that in adopting a plant or animal eponym a social unit does not make an implicit affirmation of an affinity of substance between it and itself, e.g., that the group is descended from it, that it participates in its nature, or that it is sustained by it. The connection is not arbitrary; neither is it a relation of contiguity. There remains the possibility, which Firth and Fortes have glimpsed, that the relation is based on a perception of a resemblance. We then have to find out in what this resemblance consists, and on what level it is apprehended. Can we say, with the authors whom we have just quoted, that it is of a physical or moral order, thus transposing Malinowski's empiricism from the organic and affective plane to that of perception and judgment?

We may first note that the interpretation is conceivable only in the case of societies which separate the totemic from the genealogical series: though an equal importance is assigned to them, one may evoke the other because they are not connected. But in Australia they are merged, and the intuitively perceived resemblance which Fortes and Firth call into consideration would be inconceivable by the very fact of this contiguity. In very many of the tribes of North and South America, on the other hand, no resemblance at all is postulated, either implicitly or explicitly; the connection between ancestors and animals is external and historical, they came to be known, encountered, fought against, or associated with. The same is related in many African myths, including the Tallensi. All these facts lead one to search for a connection on a far more general level, a procedure which the authors we have been discussing could scarcely object to, since the connection which they themselves suggest is purely inferential.

In the second place, the hypothesis has a very restricted field of application. Firth adopts it for Polynesia because of the reported preference there for animal totems; and Fortes admits that it holds primarily for certain animals with fangs. But what is to be done with the others, and what about plants, where it is these that are more important? What, finally, of natural phenomena or objects, normal or pathological states, or manufactured objects, all of which may serve as totems and which play a part which is certainly not negligible, and is sometimes even essential, in certain Australian and Indian forms of totemism?

In other words, the interpretation offered by Firth and by Fortes is narrow in two senses. Firstly, it is limited to cultures with a highly developed ancestor cult, as well as a social structure of totemic type; secondly, among these, it is limited to mainly animal forms of totemism, or is even restricted to certain types of animals. Now we shall never get to the bottom of the alleged problem of totemism—and on this point we are in agreement with Radcliffe-Brown—by thinking up a solution having only a limited field of application and then manipulating recalcitrant cases until the facts give way, but by reaching directly a level so general that all observed cases may figure in it as particular modes.

Lastly and above all, Fortes's psychological theory is based on an incomplete analysis. It is possible that the animals, from a certain point of view, are roughly comparable to the ancestors. But this is not a necessary condition, nor is it a sufficient condition. If we may be allowed the expression, *it is not the resemblances, but the differences, which resemble each other.* By this we mean that there are not, first, animals which resemble each other (because they all share animal behavior), then ancestors which resemble each other (because they all share ancestral behavior), and lastly an overall resemblance between the two groups; but on the one hand there are animals which differ from each other (in that they belong to distinct species, each of which has its own physical appearance and mode of life), and on the other there are men—among whom the ancestors form a particular case—who also differ from each other (in that they are distributed among different segments of the society, each occupying a particular position in the social structure). The resemblance presupposed by so-called totemic representations is *between these two systems of differences.* Firth and Fortes have taken a great step in passing from a point of view centered on *subjective utility* to one of *objective analogy.* But, this progress having been made, it remains to effect the passage from *external analogy* to *internal homology*.

II

The idea of an objectively perceived resemblance between men and totems would constitute problem enough in the case of the Azande, who include among their totems imaginary creatures such as the crested water-snake, rainbow snake, water leopard, and the thunder beast.[6] But even among the Nuer, all of whose totems correspond to real objects, it has to be recognized that the list forms a rather bizarre assortment: lion, waterbuck, monitor lizard, crocodile, various snakes, tortoise, ostrich, cattle egret, durra-bird, various trees, papyrus, gourd, various fish, bee, red ant, river and stream, cattle with certain markings, monorchids, hide, rafter, rope, parts of beasts, and some diseases. Taking them as a whole, "we may say that there is no marked utilitarian element in their selection. The animals and birds and fish and plants and artifacts which are of the most use to the Nuer are absent from the list of their totems. The facts of Nuer totemism do not, therefore, support the contention of those who see in totemism chiefly, or even merely, a ritualization of empirical interests."[7]

The argument is expressly directed against Radcliffe-Brown, and Evans-Pritchard recalls that it had previously been formulated by Durkheim with regard to similar theories. What follows may be applied to the interpretation offered by Firth and by Fortes: "Nor in general are Nuer totems such creatures as might be expected, on account of some striking peculiarities, to attract particular attention. On the contrary, those creatures which have excited the mythopoeic imagination of the Nuer and which figure most prominently in their folk-tales do not figure, or figure rarely and insignificantly, among their totems."[8]

The author declines therefore to answer the question—constantly encountered like a *Leitmotiv* from the beginning of our exposition—why it is that mammals, birds, reptiles, and trees should be symbols of the relationships between spiritual power and the lineages. The farthest he goes is to observe that certain widely held beliefs might prepare certain things to fill this function: e.g., birds fly, and are thus better able to communicate with the supreme spirit who lives in the sky. The argument does not apply to snakes, even though they are also, in their way, manifestations of Spirit. Trees, rare on the savannah, are regarded as divine favors, because of the shade they afford; rivers and streams are related to water spirits. As for monorchids and animals with certain markings, it is believed that they are visible signs of an exceptionally powerful spiritual activity.

Unless we return to an empiricism and a naturalism which Evans-Pritchard rightly rejects, it has to be recognized that these indigenous ideas are not very significant. For if we exclude the possibility that streams are the objects of ritual attitudes because of their biological or economic function, their supposed relationship with the water spirits is reduced to a purely verbal manner of expressing the spiritual value which is attributed to them, which is not an explanation. The same applies to the other cases. On the other hand, Evans-Pritchard has been able to make profound analyses which allow him to dismantle bit by bit, as it were, the relations which, in Nuer thought, unite certain types of men to certain species of animals.

In order to characterize twins, the Nuer employ expressions which at first sight seem contradictory. On the one hand, they say that twins are "one person" (*ran*); on the other, they state that twins are not "persons" (*ran*), but "birds" (*dit*). To interpret these expressions correctly, it is necessary to envisage, step by step, the reasoning involved. As manifestations of spiritual power, twins are firstly "children of God" (*gat kwoth*), and since the sky is the divine abode they may also be called "persons of the above" (*ran nhial*). In this context they are opposed to ordinary humans, who are "persons of below" (*ran piny*). As birds are themselves "of the above," twins are assimilated to them.

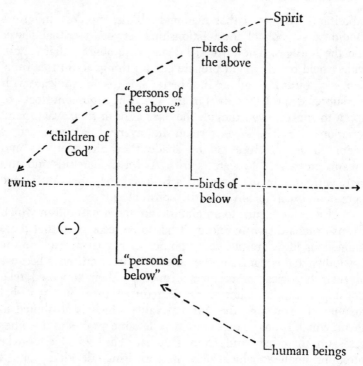

However, twins remain human beings: although they are "of the above," they are relatively "of below." But the same distinction applies to birds, since certain species fly less high and less well than others: in their own sphere, consequently, while remaining generally "of the above," birds may also be divided according to above and below. We may thus understand why twins are called by the names of "terrestrial" birds: guinea fowl, francolin, etc.

The relation thus postulated between twins and birds is explained neither by a principle of participation after the manner of Lévy-Bruhl, nor by utilitarian considerations such as those adduced by Malinowski, nor by the intuition of perceptible resemblances proposed by Firth and by Fortes. What we are presented with is a series of logical connections uniting mental relations. Twins "are birds," not because they are confused with

them or because they look like them, but because twins, in relation to other men, are as "persons of the above" to "persons of
below," and, in relation to birds, as "birds of below" are to
"birds of the above." They thus occupy, as do birds, an intermediary position between the supreme spirit and human beings.

Although it is not explicitly set out by Evans-Pritchard, this
reasoning leads him to an important conclusion. For this kind
of inference is applicable not only to the particular relationships
which the Nuer establish between twins and birds (which are
closely paralleled, moreover, by those which the Kwakiutl of
British Columbia conceive of between twins and salmon, a comparison which in itself suggests that in both cases the process is
based on a more general principle), but to every relationship
postulated between human groups and animal species. As Evans-
Pritchard himself says, this relation is metaphorical.[9] The Nuer
speak about natural species by analogy with their own social
segments such as lineages, and the relation between a lineage and
a totemic species is conceptualized on the model of what they
call *buth*, the relationship between collateral lineages descended
from a common ancestor. The animal world is thus thought of in
terms of the social world. There is the community (*cieng*) of
carnivorous animals—lion, leopard, hyena, jackal, wild dog and
domestic dog—which includes as one of its lineages (*thok dwiel*)
the mongooses, which are subdivided into a number of smaller
lineages of little animals (several varieties of mongooses and the
lesser felines, etc.). Another collectivity or class or kind (*bab*)
is formed of graminivorous animals: antelopes, gazelles, buffaloes,
and cows, and also hares, sheep, goats, etc. That of "the feetless
people" groups the lineages of snakes, and "the river people"
unites all animals which live in streams and marshes, such as
crocodiles, monitor lizards, all fish, marsh birds and fisher-birds,
as well as, furthermore, the Anuak and Balak Dinka peoples,
who for the most part are without cattle and are riverain cultiva-
tors and fishermen. Birds form a vast community subdivided into
a number of lineages: "children of God," "sister's sons of the
children of God," and "sons or daughters of aristocrats." [10]

These theoretical classifications are the basis of the totemic ideas:

> An interpretation of the totemic relationship is here, then, not to be sought in the nature of the totem itself but in an association it brings to the mind.[11]

Evans-Pritchard has recently reformulated this view more rigorously:

> On to the creatures are posited conceptions and sentiments derived from elsewhere than from them.[12]

However fertile these views may be, they are nevertheless subject to reserve in two respects. In the first place, the native theory of twins is too strictly subordinated to Nuer theology: "The formula [assimilating twins to birds] does not express a dyadic relationship between twins and birds but a triadic relationship between twins, birds, and God. With respect to God twins and birds have a similar character." [13]

But a belief in a supreme deity is not necessary to the establishment of relations of this type, and we have ourselves demonstrated them for societies much less theologically minded than the Nuer.* In formulating his interpretation in this way, Evans-Pritchard thus runs the risk of restricting it: like Firth and Fortes (though to a lesser degree), he presents a general interpretation in the language of a particular society, thus limiting its scope.

In the second place, Evans-Pritchard seems not to have appreciated the importance of the revolution achieved by Radcliffe-Brown, some years before the publication of *Nuer Religion*, with his second theory of totemism.† The latter differs from the

---

* Compare the scheme on p. 80 above with that which we present in "La Geste d'Asdiwal," *Annuaire* (1958-1959) *de l'École Pratique des Hautes Études,* Section des Sciences Religieuses, p. 20; republished in *Les Temps modernes,* No. 179, March 1961, p. 1099.

† In 1960 Evans-Pritchard still seemed to think that Radcliffe-Brown's contribution to the problem of totemism was confined to his 1929 article (Evans-Pritchard, 1960, p. 19 n. 1).

first far more radically than English anthropologists seem to realize. In our opinion, it not only completes the liquidation of the problem of totemism, but it brings out the real problem, one which is posed at another level and in different terms and which until then had not been clearly perceived, though in the final analysis its presence may be taken to be the fundamental cause of the intense eddies produced by totemism in anthropological thought. It would scarcely be credible, indeed, that numerous and capable minds should have been so exercised without a reasonable motive, even if the state of knowledge and tenacious prejudices prevented them from realizing what it was, or revealed it to them only in a deformed aspect. We have now to turn our attention, therefore, to Radcliffe-Brown's second theory.

III

This theory appeared twenty-two years after the first, without the author emphasizing its novelty, in the Huxley Memorial Lecture for 1951 entitled "The Comparative Method in Social Anthropology." In fact, Radcliffe-Brown offers it as an example of this comparative method which alone will permit anthropology to formulate "general propositions." This is the same way in which the first theory was introduced.[14] There is thus a methodological continuity between the one and the other. But the resemblance ends there.

The Australian tribes of the Darling River, in New South Wales, are divided into matrilineal exogamous moieties called Eaglehawk and Crow. A historical explanation for such a social system may be sought, e.g., that two hostile peoples once decided to make peace, and to secure it agreed that thenceforth the men of one group should marry women of the other, and reciprocally. But as we know nothing about the past of the tribes in question, this kind of explanation is condemned to remain gratuitous and conjectural.

Let us see rather whether similar institutions exist elsewhere. The Haida, of the Queen Charlotte Islands in British Columbia, are divided into matrilineal exogamous moieties called

Eagle and Raven. A Haida myth tells how, at the beginning of time, the eagle was the master of all the water on the earth, which he kept in a water-tight basket. The raven stole the basket, but as he flew with it over the island the water spilled on to the earth, thus creating the lakes and rivers from which the birds have since drunk and where came the salmon on which men chiefly live.

The eponymous birds of these Australian and American moieties thus belong to very similar, and symmetrically opposed, species. Moreover, there is an Australian myth which very much resembles the one just related. In this, the eaglehawk formerly kept the water in a well that he kept closed with a large stone, and which he lifted when he wanted to drink. The crow discovered this subterfuge, and, wanting to have a drink himself, lifted the stone: he scratched his head, which was full of lice, over the water, and forgot to replace the stone. All the water ran away, forming the rivers of eastern Australia, and the lice changed into the fish which the natives eat. Ought we then to imagine, in the spirit of historical reconstruction, that there were formerly connections between Australia and America, in order to explain these analogies?

This would be to forget that Australian exogamous moieties —both matrilineal and patrilineal—are frequently designated by the names of birds, and that consequently, in Australia itself, the Darling River tribes are merely an illustration of a general situation. The white cockatoo is opposed to the crow in Western Australia, and white cockatoo to black cockatoo in Victoria. Bird totems are also very widespread in Melanesia, e.g., the moieties of certain tribes of New Ireland are named after the sea-eagle and the fish-hawk. To generalize further, we may compare the facts recounted earlier in connection with sexual totemism (and no longer with moieties), which also employs bird or animal designations: in eastern Australia the bat is the masculine totem, the night owl the feminine; in the northern part of New South Wales the totems are respectively the bat and the tree-creeper (*Climacteris sp.*). Finally, it happens that the Australian dualism is also applied to generations, i.e., an individual is placed in the same category as his grandfather and his grandson, while his father and his son are assigned to the opposite category. The moieties by generations thus formed are usually not given names. But where they are, they may be known by the names of birds, e.g., in western Australia, as kingfisher and bee-eater, or little red bird and little black bird.

Our question "Why all these birds?" is thus widened in its scope. It is not only the exogamous moieties, but also dual divisions of other kinds that are identified by connection with a pair of birds. It is, however, not always a question of birds. In Australia the moieties may be associated with other pairs of animals, with two species of kangaroo in one part, with two species of bee in another. In California one moiety is associated with the coyote and the other with the wild cat.[15]

The comparative method consists precisely in integrating a particular phenomenon into a larger whole, which the progress of the comparison makes more and more general. In conclusion, we are confronted with the following problem: how may it be explained that social groups, or segments of society, should be distinguished from each other by the association of each with a particular natural species? This, which is the very problem of totemism, includes two others: how does each society see the relationship between human beings and the other natural species (a problem which is external to totemism, as the Andaman example shows); and how does it come about, on the other hand, that social groups should be identified by means of emblems or symbols, or by emblematic or symbolic objects? This second problem lies equally outside the framework of totemism, since in this regard the same role may be vested, according to the type of community considered, in a flag, a coat of arms, a saint, or an animal species.

So far, Radcliffe-Brown's analysis has reproduced that which he formulated in 1929, which corresponds closely, as we have seen, with that of Boas.[16] But his address of 1951 makes an innovation in declaring that this is not enough, for there remains an unresolved problem. Even if we assume that we can offer a satisfactory explanation of the "totemic" predilection for animal species, we still have to try to understand why any particular species is selected rather than another:

What is the principle by which such pairs as eaglehawk and crow, eagle and raven, coyote and wild cat are chosen as representing the moieties of the dual division? The reason for asking this question is not idle curiosity. We may, it can be held, suppose that an understanding of the principle in question will give us an important insight into the way in which the natives themselves think about the dual division as a part of their social structure. In other words, instead of asking "Why all these birds?" we can ask "Why particularly eaglehawk and crow, and other pairs?".[17]

This step is decisive. It brings about a reintegration of content with form, and thus opens the way to a genuine structural analysis, equally far removed from formalism and from functionalism. For it is indeed a structural analysis which Radcliffe-Brown undertakes, consolidating institutions with representations on the one hand, and interpreting in conjunction all the variants of the same myth on the other.

This myth, which is known from many parts of Australia, has to do with two protagonists, whose conflicts are the principal theme of the story. One version from Western Australia is about Eaglehawk and Crow. The former is mother's brother to Crow, and his potential father-in-law also because of the preferential marriage with the mother's brother's daughter. A father-in-law, real or potential, has the right to demand presents of food from his son-in-law and nephew, and Eaglehawk accordingly tells Crow to bring him a wallaby. After a successful hunt, Crow succumbs to temptation: he eats the animal and pretends to return empty-handed. But the uncle refuses to believe him, and questions him about his distended belly. Crow answers that to stay the pangs of his hunger he had filled his belly with the gum from the acacia. Still disbelieving him, Eaglehawk tickles his nephew until he vomits the meat. As a punishment, he throws him into the fire and keeps him there until his eyes are red and his feathers are blackened, while he emits in his pain the cry which is henceforth to be characteristic. Eaglehawk pronounces that Crow shall never again be a hunter, and that he will be reduced to stealing game. This is the way things have been ever since.

It is impossible, Radcliffe-Brown continues, to understand this myth without reference to the ethnographic context. The Australian aborigine thinks of himself as a "meat-eater," and the eaglehawk and crow, which are carnivorous birds, are his main rivals. When the natives go hunting by lighting bush-fires, the eaglehawks quickly appear and join in the hunt: they also are hunters. Perching not far from the camp fires, the crows await their chance to steal from the feast.

Myths of this type may be compared with others, the structure of which is similar, although they are concerned with different animals. For example, the aborigines who inhabit the region where South Australia joins Victoria say that the kangaroo and the wombat (another marsupial, but smaller), which are the principal game, were once friends. One day Wombat began to make a "house" for himself (the animal lives in a burrow in the ground), and Kangaroo jeered at him and thus annoyed him. But when, for the very first time, rain began to fall, and Wombat sheltered in his house, he refused to make room for Kangaroo, claiming that it was too small for two. Furious, Kangaroo struck Wombat on the head with a big stone, flattening his skull; and Wombat, in riposte, threw a spear at Kangaroo which fixed itself at the base of the backbone. This is the way things have been ever since: the wombat has a flat skull and lives in a burrow; the kangaroo has a tail and lives in the open: "This is, of course, a 'just-so' story which you may think is childish. It amuses the listeners when it is told with the suitable dramatic expressions. But if we examine some dozens of these tales we find that they have a single theme. The resemblances and differences of animal species are translated into terms of friendship and conflict, solidarity and opposition. In other words the world of animal life is represented in terms of social relations similar to those of human society." [18]

To arrive at this end, the natural species are classed in pairs of opposites, and this is possible only on condition that the species chosen have in common at least one characteristic which permits them to be compared.

The principle is clear in the case of the eaglehawk and crow, which are the two main carnivorous birds, though they differ from each other in that one is a bird of prey and the other a carrion-eater. But how are we to interpret the pair bat/night owl? Radcliffe-Brown admits that at first he was misled by the fact that both fly about at night. However, in one part of New South Wales it is the tree-creeper, a diurnal bird, which is opposed to the bat; it is the feminine totem, and a myth relates that it is this bird which taught women to climb trees.

Encouraged by this first explanation supplied by his informant, Radcliffe-Brown then asked, "What resemblance is there between the bat and the tree-creeper?" The native, obviously surprised by such ignorance, answered, "But of course they both live in holes in trees." This is also the case with the night owl and the nightjar. To eat meat, or to live in trees, is the common feature of the pair considered and presents a point of comparison with the human condition.* But there is also an opposition within the pair, underlying the similarity: while both of the birds are carnivorous, one is a "hunter" and the other is a "thief." While they are members of the same species, cockatoos differ in color, being white or black; birds which similarly live in holes in trees are distinguished as diurnal and nocturnal, and so on.

Consequently, the division eaglehawk/crow among the Darling River tribes, with which we began, is seen at the end of the analysis to be no more than "one particular example of a widespread type of the application of a certain structural principle," [19] a principle consisting of the union of opposites. The

---

* As we have gone a little beyond Radcliffe-Brown's account it may be asked in what respect the life of birds which live in holes in trees recalls the human condition. There is at least one Australian tribe, as a matter of fact, which names its moieties after the parts of a tree: "In the Ngeumba tribe Gwaimudthen is divided into nhurai (butt) and wangue (middle), while Gwaigulir is equivalent to winggo (top). These names refer to different portions of the shadow of a tree and refer to the positions taken up in camping. . . ." (Thomas, 1906, p. 152).

alleged totemism is no more than a particular expression, by means of a special nomenclature formed of animal and plant names (in a certain code, as we should say today), which is its sole distinctive characteristic, of correlations and oppositions which may be formalized in other ways, e.g., among certain tribes of North and South America, by oppositions of the type sky/earth, war/peace, upstream/downstream, red/white, etc. The most general model of this, and the most systematic application, is to be found perhaps in China, in the opposition of the two principles of Yang and Yin, as male and female, day and night, summer and winter, the union of which results in an organized totality (*tao*) such as the conjugal pair, the day, or the year. Totemism is thus reduced to a particular fashion of formulating a general problem, viz., how to make opposition, instead of being an obstacle to integration, serve rather to produce it.

IV

Radcliffe-Brown's demonstration ends decisively the dilemma in which the adversaries as well as the proponents of totemism have been trapped because they could assign only two roles to living species, viz., that of a natural stimulus, or that of an arbitrary pretext. The animals in totemism cease to be solely or principally creatures which are feared, admired, or envied: their perceptible reality permits the embodiment of ideas and relations conceived by speculative thought on the basis of empirical observations. We can understand, too, that natural species are chosen not because they are "good to eat" but because they are "good to think."

The gap between this thesis and its predecessor is so great that we should like to know whether Radcliffe-Brown appreciated it. The answer is perhaps to be found in the notes of lectures he delivered in South Africa, and in the unpublished manuscript of an address on Australian cosmology, the last occasions for the expression of his thought before he died in 1953. He was not the man to admit with good grace that he might change his mind, or to recognize possible influences. Yet it is difficult not to remark, in this respect, that the ten years which preceded his Huxley Memorial Lecture were marked by the drawing together of anthropology and structural linguistics. For those who took part in this enterprise it is tempting at least to think that this may have found an echo in Radcliffe-Brown's thought. The ideas of opposition and correlation, and that of pair of opposites, have a long history; but it is structural linguistics and subsequently structural anthropology which rehabilitated them in the vocabulary of the humane sciences. It is striking to meet them, with all their implications, in the writings of Radcliffe-Brown, who, as we have seen, was led by them to abandon his earlier positions, which were still stamped with the mark of naturalism and empiricism. This departure, nevertheless, was not made without hesitation, and at one point Radcliffe-Brown seems uncertain about the scope of his thesis and the extent of its application beyond the area of the Australian facts: "The Australian idea of what is here called 'opposition' is a particular application of that association by contrariety that is a universal feature of human thinking, so that we think by pairs of contraries, upwards and downwards, strong and weak, black and white. But the Australian conception of 'opposition' combines the idea of a pair of contraries with that of a pair of opponents." [20]

It is certainly the case that one consequence of modern structuralism (not, however, clearly enunciated) ought to be to rescue associational psychology from the discredit into which it has fallen. Associationism had the great merit of sketching the contours of this elementary logic, which is like the least common denominator of all thought, and its only failure was not to recognize that it was an original logic, a direct expression of the structure of the mind (and behind the mind, probably, of the brain), and not an inert product of the action of the environment on an amorphous consciousness. But, contrary to what Radcliffe-Brown tends still to believe, it is this logic of oppositions and correlations, exclusions and inclusions, compatibilities and incompatibilities, which explains the laws of association, not the reverse. A renovated associationism would have to be based on a system of operations which would not be without similarity to Boolean algebra. As Radcliffe-Brown's very conclusions demonstrate, his analysis of Australian facts guides him beyond a simple ethnographic generalization—to the laws of language, and even of thought.

Nor is this all. We have already remarked that Radcliffe-Brown understood that in a structural analysis it is impossible to dissociate form from content. The form is not outside, but inside. In order to perceive the rationale of animal designations they must be envisaged concretely, for we are not free to trace a boundary on the far side of which purely arbitrary considerations would reign. Meaning is not decreed: if it is not everywhere it is nowhere. It is true that our limited knowledge often prevents us from pursuing it to its last retreats; for instance, Radcliffe-Brown does not explain why certain Australian tribes conceptualize the affinity between animal life and the human condition by analogy with carnivorous tastes while other tribes frame it in terms of common habitat. But his analysis implicitly presupposes that this difference itself is also meaningful, and that if we were better informed we should be able to correlate it with other differences, to be discovered between the respective beliefs of two groups, between their techniques, or between the relations of each to its environment.

In fact, the method adopted by Radcliffe-Brown is as sound as the interpretations which it suggests to him. Each level of social reality appears to him as an indispensable complement, without which it would be impossible to understand the other levels. Customs lead to beliefs, and these lead to techniques, but the different levels do not simply reflect each other. They react dialectically among themselves in such a way that we cannot hope to understand one of them without first evaluating, through their respective relations of opposition and correlation, *institutions, representations,* and *situations.* In every one of its practical undertakings, anthropology thus does no more than assert a homology of structure between human thought in action and the human object to which it is applied. The methodological integration of essence and form reflects, in its own way, a more necessary integration—that between method and reality.

FIVE

Totemism from Within

I

Radcliffe-Brown would probably have rejected the conclusions which we have just drawn from his analysis, for until the end of his life, and as is proved by a correspondence with him,[*] he held fast to an empiricist conception of structure. However, we believe that we have delineated, without distorting it, the attractiveness of one of the paths opened up by his address of 1951. Even if he himself might not have taken it, it bears witness to the fertility of a mind which, age and illness notwithstanding, still showed its capacity for revival.

Novel though Radcliffe-Brown's second theory of totemism may appear in anthropological literature, he is not, however, its inventor; yet it is scarcely probable that he should have been inspired by predecessors who were quite marginal to strictly anthropological speculation. Considering the intellectualist character that we have discerned in his theory, we might be surprised that Bergson should have held very similar ideas. Yet we find in *Les Deux Sources de la morale et de la religion* the outline of a theory which in certain respects presents an analogy with Radcliffe-Brown's which it is interesting to examine. This also offers occasion to pose a problem concerning the history of ideas, one which takes us back to the postulates implied by speculations on totemism, viz., how is it that a philosopher known for the importance he attached to affectivity and experience should find himself, in approaching an anthropological problem, at the opposite pole to those anthropologists whose theoretical position may be considered so close to his in all other respects?

[*] See Radcliffe-Brown's letter to the author, published in *An Appraisal of Anthropology Today*, ed. S. Tax et al., Chicago, 1953, p. 109.

In *Les Deux Sources,* Bergson approaches totemism indirectly, by way of animal worship, which he regards as a form of spirit cult. Totemism is not to be confused with zoolatry, but it presupposes all the same that "man treats an animal, or even vegetable, species, and sometimes an inanimate object, with a deference that is not entirely dissimilar to religion."[1] This deference seems to be connected in native thought to the belief in an identity between the animal or plant and the members of the clan. How may this belief be explained?

The gamut of interpretations proposed range themselves between two extreme hypotheses: one a "participation," after Lévy-Bruhl, which treats in cavalier fashion the multiple meanings of expressions in different languages which we translate by the verb "to be," the meaning of which is equivocal even among ourselves; the other, a reduction of the totem to the role of emblem and simple designation of the clan, which is what Durkheim does, but without then being able to account for the place occupied by totemism in the life of the peoples that practice it.

Neither the one interpretation nor the other permits us to answer simply and unequivocally the question posed by the clear predilection for animal and vegetable species. We are thus led to inquire what there is that is distinctive in the way man perceives and conceptualizes plants and animals:

At the same time as the nature of the animal seems to be concentrated into a unique quality, we might say that its individuality is dissolved in a genus. To recognise a man means to distinguish him from other men; but to recognise an animal is normally to decide what species it belongs to. . . . An animal lacks concreteness and individuality, it appears essentially as a quality, and thus essentially as a class.[2]

It is this direct perception of the *class,* through the individuals, which characterizes the relation between man and the animal or plant, and it is this also which helps us to understand "this singular thing that is totemism." In fact, the truth must be sought halfway between the two extreme solutions recalled above:

There is nothing to be deduced from the fact that a clan is said to be one or other animal; but that two clans of the same tribe have necessarily to be two different animals is far more enlightening. Let us suppose that it is desired to mark the fact that these two clans constitute two species, in the biological sense of the word, . . . giving one the name of one animal and the other the name of another. Each of these names, taken by itself, is nothing but an appellation, but together they are equivalent to an affirmation. They say, in fact, that the two clans are of *different blood*.[3]

There is no need for us to follow Bergson to the very end of his theory, for there we should be led onto less solid ground. Bergson sees totemism as a means of exogamy, this itself being the effect of an instinct intended to prevent biologically harmful unions between close relatives. But if such an instinct existed, a recourse to institutions would be superfluous. Moreover, the sociological model adopted would be in curious contradiction with the zoological situation which inspired it: animals are endogamous, not exogamous; they come together and reproduce exclusively within the limits of the species. In "specifying" each clan, and in differentiating them "specifically" from each other, the result—if totemism were based on biological tendencies and natural feelings—would be the reverse of that intended: i.e., each clan would have to be endogamous, like a biological species, and the clans would remain strangers to each other.

Bergson is so aware of these difficulties that he hastens to modify his thesis on two counts. While still maintaining the reality of the need which should constrain people to avoid consanguineous unions, he concedes that there is no "real and active" instinct corresponding to it. Nature supplies this lack by means of intelligence, arousing "an imaginative representation which determines behaviour as the instinct might have done." [4] But, aside from the fact that this leads to a pure metaphysic, this "imaginative representation" would still have, as we have just seen, a content exactly the opposite of its alleged object. It is probably in order to get round this second difficulty that Bergson is forced to reduce an imaginative representation to a form:

When, therefore, they [the members of two clans] declare that they are two species of animals, it is not on the animality but on the duality that they place the stress.[5]

In spite of the difference between their premises, it is Radcliffe-Brown's very conclusion which Bergson enunciates, and twenty years before him.

II

This perspicacity of the philosopher, which imposes on him, even against his reluctance, the correct answer to an anthropological problem still unsolved by professional anthropologists (*Les Deux Sources* was published not long after Radcliffe-Brown's first theory) is the more remarkable in that a theoretical change-over is produced between Bergson and Durkheim, who were contemporaries. The philosopher of the unstable finds the solution to the problem of totemism in the field of oppositions and ideas; while by a move in the opposite direction Durkheim, inclined though he always was to refer back to categories and even to antinomies, seeks the answer at the level of indistinction. Actually, the Durkheimian theory of totemism is developed in three stages, of which Bergson, in his criticism, is content to retain the first two. The clan first gives itself an emblem "instinctively," [6] which can only be a sketchy figure limited to a few lines. Later, an animal figure is "recognized" in the design, and it is changed in consequence. Finally this figure is sacralized, by a sentimental confusion of the clan and its emblem.

But how can this series of operations, which each clan carries out on its own account and independently of the other clans, be organized eventually into a system? Durkheim replies:

If the totemic principle resides by choice in a particular animal or vegetable, it cannot remain localised in it. The sacred is contagious in the extreme; it thus extends from the totemic being to everything that is at all connected with it . . . : the things it feeds on, . . . things that resemble it, . . . various beings with which it is constantly connected. . . . At last, the whole world is shared between the totemic principles of the same tribe.[7]

The term "shared" is clearly ambiguous, for a true sharing would not result in a mutual and unforseen limitation of areas of expansion, each of which would invade the entire field unless it were prevented by the advances of the others. The distribution which would result would be arbitrary and contingent, resulting from history and chance; and it would be impossible to understand how passively experienced distinctions, submitted to without ever having been conceptualized, could be at the origin of those "primitive classifications" whose systematic and coherent character Durkheim, together with Mauss, had established:

It is far from being the case that this mentality has no connexion with our own. Our logic was born of this logic. . . . Today, as in former times, to explain is to show how a thing participates in one or a number of others . . . Every time we unite heterogeneous terms by an internal link we necessarily identify contraries. Of course, the terms that we unite in this way are not those that the Australian brings together; we choose them by other criteria and for other reasons; but the process itself by which the mind relates them does not differ essentially. . . .

Thus there is no abyss between the logic of religious thought and the logic of scientific thought. Both are composed of the same essential elements, only unequally and differently developed. The special characteristic of the former seems to be its natural taste for immoderate confusions as well as for abrupt contrasts. It is willingly excessive in both directions. When it compares, it confuses; when it distinguishes, it opposes. It knows neither measure nor subtlety, it seeks extremes; consequently it employs logical mechanisms with a kind of awkwardness, but it is ignorant of none of them.[8]

If we have quoted these lines at some length, it is firstly because they are Durkheim at his best, i.e., he is admitting that all social life, even elementary, presupposes an intellectual activity in man of which the formal properties, consequently, cannot be a reflection of the concrete organization of the society. But the theme of *Les Formes élémentaires de la vie religieuse*, like what we might extract from the second preface to *Les Règles de la méthode sociologique* and from the essay on primitive forms of classification, shows the contradictions inherent in the contrary view, which is only too often adopted by Durkheim when he affirms the primacy of the social over the intellect. Now it is precisely to the degree that Bergson intends the opposite of the sociologist, in the Durkheimian sense of the word, that he is able to make the category of class and the notion of opposition into immediate data of the understanding, which are utilized by the social order in its formation. And it is when Durkheim claims to derive categories and abstract ideas from the social order that, in trying to explain this order, he finds at his disposal no more than sentiments, affective values, or vague ideas such as contagion or contamination. His thought thus remains torn between two contradictory claims. This explains the paradox, well illustrated by the history of the totemic issue, that Bergson is in a better position than Durkheim to lay the foundations of a genuine sociological logic, and that Durkheim's psychology, as much as Bergson's but in the opposite direction, has to call upon the inarticulate.

So far, the Bergsonian procedure seems to be made up of a succession of retreats, as though Bergson, forced to break off in the face of each of the objections raised by his thesis, had been driven into a corner in spite of himself, with his back to the truth of totemism. But this interpretation does not go to the bottom of the matter, for it may be that Bergson's insight was due to more positive and profound reasons. If he was able to understand certain aspects of totemism better than the anthropologists, or before them, is this not because his own thought presents curious analogies with that of many so-called primitive peoples who experience or have experienced totemism from within?

For the anthropologist, Bergson's philosophy recalls irresistibly that of the Sioux, and he himself could have remarked the similarity since he had read and pondered *Les Formes élémentaires de la vie religieuse*. Durkheim reproduces in this book[9] a reflection by a Dakota wise man which formulates, in a language close to that of *L'Évolution créatrice*, a metaphysical philosophy, common to all the Sioux, from the Osage in the south to the Dakota in the north, according to which things and beings are nothing but materialized forms of creative continuity. The original American source reads:

Everything as it moves, now and then, here and there, makes stops. The bird as it flies stops in one place to make its nest, and in another to rest in its flight. A man when he goes forth stops when he wills. So the god has stopped. The sun, which is so bright and beautiful, is one place where he has stopped. The moon, the stars, the winds, he has been with. The trees, the animals, are all where he has stopped, and the Indian thinks of these places and sends his prayers there to reach the place where the god has stopped and win help and a blessing.[10]

The better to underline the comparison, let us quote without break from the paragraph in *Les Deux Sources* where Bergson sums up his metaphysics:

A great current of creative energy gushes forth through matter, to obtain from it what it can. At most points it is stopped; these stops are transmuted, in our eyes, into the appearances of so many living species, i.e., of organisms in which our perception, being essentially analytical and synthetic, distinguishes a multitude of elements combining to fulfill a multitude of functions; but the process of organisation was only the stop itself, a simple act analogous to the impress of a foot which instantaneously causes thousands of grains of sand to contrive to form a pattern.[11]

The two accounts agree so exactly that it may seem less risky, after reading them, to claim that Bergson was able to understand what lay behind totemism because his own thought, unbeknownst to him, was in sympathy with that of totemic peoples. What is it, then, that they have in common? It seems that the relationship results from one and the same desire to apprehend in a total fashion the two aspects of reality which the philosopher terms *continuous* and *discontinuous*; from the same refusal to choose between the two; and from the same effort to see them as complementary perspectives giving on to the same truth.* Radcliffe-Brown, though abstaining from metaphysical considerations which were foreign to his temperament, followed the same route, when he reduced totemism to a particular form of a universal tendency, in order to reconcile *opposition* and *integration*. This encounter between a fieldworker admirably aware of the way in which savages think, and an armchair philosopher who in certain respects thinks like a savage, could only be produced by a fundamental matter which needed to be dealt with.

Radcliffe-Brown had a more distant predecessor, and one hardly less unexpected, in the person of Jean-Jacques Rousseau. Certainly, Rousseau felt a much more militant fervor for ethnography than Bergson; but, aside from the fact that ethnographic knowledge was far more limited in the eighteenth century, what makes Rousseau's insight more astonishing is that it forestalls by a number of years the very first ideas about totemism. It will be recalled that these were introduced by Long, whose book was published in 1791, whereas the *Discours sur l'origine de l'inégalité* goes back to 1754. Yet Rousseau, like Radcliffe-Brown and Bergson, sees the apprehension by man of the "specific" character of the animal and vegetable world as the source of the first logical operations, and subsequently of a social differentiation which could be lived out only if it were conceptualized.

The *Discours sur l'origine et les fondements de l'inégalité parmi les hommes* is without doubt the first anthropological treatise in French literature. In almost modern terms, Rousseau poses the central problem of anthropology, viz., the passage from nature to culture. More prudently than Bergson, he abstains from introducing the idea of instinct, which, belonging as it does to the order of nature, could not enable him to go beyond nature. Before man became a social being, the instinct of procreation, "a blind urge, . . . produced no more than a purely animal act."

---

* The analogy deserves to be pursued. The Dakota language possesses no word to designate time, but it can express in a number of ways modes of being in duration. For Dakota thought, in fact, time constitutes a duration in which measurement does not intervene: it is a limitless "free good" (Malan and McCone, 1960, p. 12).

The passage from nature to culture depended on demographic increase, but the latter did not produce a direct effect, as a natural cause. First it forced men to diversify their modes of livelihood in order to exist in different environments, and also to multiply their relations with nature. But in order that this diversification and multiplication might lead to technical and social transformations, they had to become objects and means of human thought:

This repeated attention of various beings to themselves and to each other must naturally have engendered in man's mind the perception of certain relations. The relations which we express by the words big and little, strong and weak, fast and slow, bold and fearful, and other such ideas which are compared as occasion demands and almost without thinking about them, eventually produced in man a kind of reflection, or rather an automatic prudence which indicated the precautions most necessary to his safety.[12]

The concluding part of the quotation is not to be explained as an afterthought: in Rousseau's view, foresight and curiosity are connected as two aspects of intellectual activity. In the state of nature, both are lacking in man, because he "abandons himself solely to the consciousness of his present existence." For Rousseau, moreover, affective life and intellectual life are opposed in the same way as nature and culture, which are as remote from each other as "pure sensations from the simplest forms of knowledge." This is true to the extent that he sometimes writes, not of the state of society, in opposition to that of nature, but of the "state of reasoning." [13]

The advent of culture thus coincides with the birth of the intellect. Furthermore, the opposition between the continuous and the discontinuous, which seems irreducible on the biological plane because it is expressed by the seriality of individuals within the species, and in the heterogeneity of the species among each other, is surmounted in culture, which is based on the aptitude of man to perfect himself, ". . . a faculty which . . . remains with us, in the species as much as in the individual; and without which an animal is, after a few months, what it will be all its life, and a species, after a thousand years, what it was in the first year of the thousand." [14]

How then are we to conceive, firstly, the triple passage (which is really only one) from animality to humanity, from nature to culture, and from affectivity to intellectuality, and, secondly, the possibility of the application of the animal and vegetable world to society, perceived already by Rousseau, and in which we see the key to totemism? For in making a radical separation between the terms one runs the risk (as Durkheim was later to learn) of no longer understanding their origin.

Rousseau's answer consists in defining the natural condition of man, while still retaining the distinctions, by the only psychic state of which the content is indissociably both affective and intellectual, and which the act of consciousness suffices to transfer from one level to the other, viz., compassion, or, as Rousseau also writes, identification with another, the duality of terms corresponding, up to a certain point, to the above duality of aspect. It is because man originally felt himself identical to all those like him (among which, as Rousseau explicitly says, we must include animals) that he came to acquire the capacity to distinguish *himself* as he distinguishes *them,* i.e., to use the diversity of species as conceptual support for social differentiation.

This philosophy of an original identification with all other creatures is as far as may be imagined from Sartre's existentialism, which on this point returns to Hobbes's view. In other respects it leads Rousseau to some singular hypotheses, such as Note 10 in the *Discours,* in which he suggests that the orang-utang and other anthropoid apes of Asia and Africa might be men, wrongly confused with animals by the prejudices of travelers. But it also enables him to form an extraordinarily modern view of the passage from nature to culture, and one based, as we have seen, on the emergence of a logic operating by means of binary oppositions and coinciding with the first manifestations of symbolism. The total apprehension of men and animals as sentient beings, in which identification consists, both governs and precedes the consciousness of oppositions between, firstly, logical properties conceived as integral parts of the field, and then, within the field itself, between "human" and "non-human." For Rousseau, this is the very development of language, the origin of which lies not in needs but in emotions, so that the first language must have been figurative:

As emotions were the first motives which induced men to speak, his first utterances were tropes. Figurative language was the first to be born, proper meanings were the last to be found. Things were called by their true name only when they were seen in their true form. The first speech was all in poetry; reasoning was thought of only long afterwards. [15]

All-enveloping terms, which confounded objects of perception and the emotions which they aroused in a kind of surreality, thus preceded analytical reduction in the strict sense. Metaphor, the role of which in totemism we have repeatedly underlined, is not a later embellishment of language but is one of its fundamental modes. Placed by Rousseau on the same plane as opposition, it constitutes, on the same ground, a primary form of discursive thought.

IV

It may seem rather a paradox that an essay concerned with the state of the totemic problem today should conclude with such retrospective considerations. But the paradox is only one aspect of the illusion of totemism, an illusion which is dissipated by a more rigorous analysis of the facts on which it was first erected, and in which what was true belongs more to the past than to the present. For the totemic illusion consists firstly in the fact that one philosopher ignorant of anthropology, as was Bergson, and another living at a time when the very idea of totemism had not been formed, should have been able, before contemporary professionals —and, in Rousseau's case, before even the "discovery" of totemism—to penetrate the nature of beliefs and customs with which they were unfamiliar, or the reality of which had not been established.

Bergson's success is undoubtedly an indirect consequence

of his philosophical assumptions. Though he was as concerned as were his contemporaries to legitimatize certain values, he differed from them in describing their limits at the heart of the normal thought of the white man instead of placing them at the periphery. The logic of distinctions and oppositions is ascribed to the savage and to the "closed society" in accordance with the inferior place assigned to it by Bergson's philosophy in comparison with other modes of understanding. The truth thus wins, as it were, "off the cushion."

But what matters to us, for the lesson we wish to draw from it, is that Bergson and Rousseau should have succeeded in getting right to the psychological foundations of exotic institutions (in the case of Rousseau, without even suspecting their existence) by a process of internalization, i.e., by trying on themselves modes of thought taken from elsewhere or simply imagined. They thus demonstrate that every human mind is a locus of virtual experience where what goes on in the minds of men, however remote they may be, can be investigated.

By the bizarre character attributed to it, and which was further exaggerated by the interpretations of ethnographers and the speculations of theorists, totemism served for a time to strengthen the case of those who tried to separate primitive institutions from our own, an effect which was particularly opportune in the case of religious phenomena, in which comparison had revealed too many obvious affinities. It is the obsession with religious matters which caused totemism to be placed in religion, though separating it as far as possible—by caricaturing it if need be—from so-called civilized religions, for fear that the latter might crumble at its touch; or else, as in Durkheim's experiment, the combination resulting in a new entity deprived of the initial properties, those of totemism as well as those of religion.

But the humane sciences can only work effectively with ideas that are clear, or which they try to make so. If it is maintained that religion constitutes an autonomous order, requiring a special kind of investigation, it has to be removed from the common fate of objects of science. Religion having thus been defined by contrast, it will inevitably appear, in the eyes of science, to be distinguished as no more than a sphere of confused ideas. Thenceforth, any attempt to make an objective study of religion will have to be directed to a domain other than that of ideas, one which has been distorted and adapted by the claims of religious anthropology. The only approach routes left open will be affective (if not actually organic) and sociological ones which will do no more than circle around the phenomena.

Conversely, if religious ideas are accorded the same value as any other conceptual system, as giving access to the mechanism of thought, the procedures of religious anthropology will acquire validity, but it will lose its autonomy and its specific character.

This is what we have seen happen in the case of totemism, the reality of which is reduced to that of a particular illustration of certain modes of thought. Sentiments are also involved, admittedly, but in a subsidiary fashion, as responses of a body of ideas to gaps and lesions which it can never succeed in closing. The alleged totemism pertains to the understanding, and the demands to which it responds and the way in which it tries to meet them are primarily of an intellectual kind. In this sense, there is nothing archaic or remote about it. Its image is projected, not received; it does not derive its substance from without. If the illusion contains a particle of truth, this is not outside us but within us.

Bibliography

The literature on totemism is enormous. This bibliography contains only publications cited in the present work.

Anthropos, "Das Problem des Totemismus," Vols. IX, X, XI, 1914-1916.

Bergson, H., *Les Deux Sources de la morale et de la religion.* 88ᵉ édition. Paris, 1958.

Best, E., "Maori Religion and Mythology," *Dominion Museum Bulletin,* No. 10, Section I, Wellington, 1924.

Boas, F., "The Origin of Totemism," *American Anthropologist,* Vol. 18, pp. 319-326, 1916.

———, ed., *General Anthropology.* Boston-New York-London.

Comte, A., *Cours de philosophie positive.* 6 vols. Paris, 1908.

Crosse-Upcott, A. R. W., "Social Aspects of Ngindo Bee-keeping," *Journal of the Royal Anthropological Institute,* Vol. 86, Part II, pp. 81-108, 1956.

Cuoq, J. A., *Lexique de la langue algonquine.* Montreal, 1886.

Dorsey, J. O., "A Study of Siouan Cults," *11th Annual Report (1889-1890), Bureau of Ethnology,* pp. 361-544. Washington, 1894.

Dumézil, G., *Loki.* Paris, 1948.

Durkheim, É., *Les Formes élémentaires de la vie religieuse.* 2ᵉ édition. Paris, 1925.

Durkheim, É. and Mauss, M., "De Quelques formes primitives de classification: contribution à l'étude des représentations collectives," *Année Sociologique,* Vol. VI, pp. 1-72, Paris, 1903. (English edition, translated and with an introduction by Rodney Needham, *Primitive Classification,* London and Chicago, 1963.)

Elkin, A. P., "Studies in Australian Totemism: Sub-section, Section, and Moiety Totemism," *Oceania,* Vol. 4 (1933-34), No. 1, pp. 65-90, 1933.

———, "Studies in Australian Totemism: The Nature of Australian Totemism," *Oceania,* Vol. 4 (1933-34), No. 2, pp. 113-131, 1933.

———, *The Australian Aborigines,* 3rd edition. Sydney-London, 1954.

Evans-Pritchard, E. E., "Zande clan names," *Man*, Vols. 56, 62, 1956.

——, "Zande totems," *Man*, Vols. 56, 110, 1956.

——, *Nuer Religion*. Oxford, 1956.

——, Introduction to Robert Hertz, *Death and the Right Hand* (trans. Rodney and Claudia Needham). London, 1960.

Firth, R., "Totemism in Polynesia," *Oceania*, Vol. I, No. 3, pp. 291-321; No. 4, pp. 378-398, 1930-31.

——, *Primitive Polynesian Economy*. London, 1939.

——, *History and Traditions of Tikopia*. Wellington, 1961.

Fortes, M., *The Dynamics of Clanship among the Tallensi*. Oxford, 1945.

Frazer, J. G., *Totemism and Exogamy*. 4 vols. London, 1910.

Freud, S., *Totem et Tabou*. Paris, 1924.

Goldenweiser, A., "Totemism, an Analytical Study," *Journal of American Folklore*, Vol. XXIII, 1910.

——, "Form and Content in Totemism," *American Anthropologist*, Vol. 20, 1918.

Handbook of American Indians North of Mexico. Bureau of American Ethnology, Smithsonian Institution, *Bulletin 30*, 2 vols. Washington, 1907-1910.

Hilger, M. I., "Some Early Customs of the Menomini Indians," *Journal de la Société des Américanistes*, Vol. XLIX (n.s.), 1960.

Jakobson, R. and Halle, M., *Fundamentals of Language*. 's-Gravenhage, 1956.

Jenness, D., "The Ojibwa Indians of Parry Island: Their Social and Religious Life," *Bulletin of the Canadian Department of Mines*, No. 78, pp. 1-115. Ottawa, 1935.

Kinietz, W. V., "Chippewa Village: The Story of Katikitegon," *Bulletin of the Cranbrook Institute of Science*, No. 25, pp. 1-259, Detroit, 1947.

Kroeber, A. L., "Totem and Taboo: An Ethnologic Psychoanalysis," (1920) reprinted in *The Nature of Culture*, pp. 301-305. Chicago, 1952.

——, *Anthropology*. New York, 1923.

——, "Totem and Taboo in Retrospect," (1939) reprinted in *The Nature of Culture*, pp. 306-309. Chicago, 1952.

——, *Anthropology*. New edition. New York, 1948.

Landes, R., "Ojibwa Sociology," *Columbia University Contributions to Anthropology*, Vol. XXIX, pp. 1-144. New York, 1937.

Lane, B. S., "Varieties of Cross-cousin Marriage and Incest Taboos:

Structure and Causality," *Essays in the Science of Culture,* ed. G. E. Dole and R. L. Carneiro, pp. 288-301. New York, 1960.

Lévi-Strauss, C., *Les Structures élémentaires de la parenté.* Paris, 1949.

————, *La Pensée Sauvage,* Paris, 1962.

Linton, R., "Totemism and the A. E. F.," *American Anthropologist,* Vol. 26, pp. 296-300, 1924.

Long, J. K., *Voyages and Travels of an Indian Interpreter and Trader* [1791], Chicago, 1922.

Lowie, R. H., "On the Principle of Convergence in Ethnology," *Journal of American Folklore,* Vol. XXV, pp. 24-42, 1912.

————, *Primitive Society.* Reprinted 1947. New York, 1920.

————, *An Introduction to Cultural Anthropology.* New York, 1934.

————, *Social Organization.* New York, 1948.

McConnel, U., "The Wik-Munkan tribe of Cape York Peninsula," *Oceania,* Vol. I, (1930-1931), No. 1, pp. 99-104; No. 2, pp. 181-205, 1930.

McLennan, J. F., "The Worship of Animals and Plants," *Fortnightly Review,* Vols. 6 and 7, 1869-1870.

Malan, V. D. and McCone, R. C., "The Time Concept Perspective and Premise in the Socio-cultural Order of the Dakota Indians," *Plains Anthropologist,* Vol. 5, 1960.

Malinowski, B., *The Sexual Life of Savages in North-western Melanesia.* 2 vols. New York-London, 1929.

————, *Magic, Science and Religion.* Boston, 1948.

Michelson, T., "Explorations and Fieldwork of the Smithsonian Institution in 1925," *Smithsonian Miscellaneous Collections,* Vol. 78, No. 1. Washington, 1926.

Murdock, G. P., *Social Structure.* New York, 1949.

Notes and Queries on Anthropology. Sixth edition. London, 1951.

Piddington, R., *An Introduction to Social Anthropology,* Vol. I. Edinburgh-London.

Prytz Johansen, J., *The Maori and His Religion and Its Non-ritualistic Aspects.* Copenhagen, 1954.

Radcliffe-Brown, A. R., "The Sociological Theory of Totemism," (1929) reprinted in *Structure and Function in Primitive Society,* pp. 117-132. London, 1952.

————, "The Social Organization of Australian Tribes," *Oceania,* Vol. I, 1930-1931.

————, "Taboo," (1939) reprinted in *Structure and Function in Primitive Society*, pp. 133-152. London, 1952.

————, "The Comparative Method in Social Anthropology," *Journal of the Royal Anthropological Institute*, Vol. 81, pp. 15-22, 1951, reprinted as Chapter V in *Method in Social Anthropology*. Chicago, 1958.

Reichard, G., "Social Life," in Boas, 1938, pp. 409-486, 1938.

Rivers, W. H. R., *The History of Melanesian Society*. 2 vols. Cambridge, 1941.

Rousseau, J.-J., *Discours sur l'origine et les fondements de l'inégalité parmi les hommes*. London, 1776.

————, *Essai sur l'origine des langues*. London, 1783.

Spencer, B. and Gillen, J., *The Northern Tribes of Central Australia*. London, 1904.

Stanner, W. E. H., "Murinbata kinship and totemism," *Oceania*, Vol. 7. 1936-1937.

Strehlow, T. G. H., *Aranda Traditions*. Melbourne, 1947.

Thomas, N. W., *Kinship Organizations and Group Marriage in Australia*. Cambridge, 1906.

Tylor, E. B., "Remarks on Totemism with Especial Reference to some Modern Theories Concerning It," *Journal of the Royal Anthropological Institute*, Vol. XXVIII, pp. 138-148. 1899.

Van Gennep, A., *L'État actuel du problème totémique*. Paris, 1920.

Werner, W. L., *A Black Civilization*. Revised edition. New York, 1958.

Warren, W., "History of the Ojibways," *Collections of the Minnesota Historical Society*, Vol. V. Saint Paul, Minn., 1885.

Zelenine, D., *Le Culte des idoles en Sibérie*. Paris, 1952.

Notes

Introduction

1. Goldenweiser, 1910.
2. Lowie, 1935, p. 151.
3. Kroeber, 1948, p. 396.
4. Reichard, 1938, p. 430.
5. Murdock, 1949, p. 50.
6. Linton, 1924, p. 298.
7. Rivers, 1914, Vol. II, p. 75.
8. Piddington, 1950, pp. 203, 204.
9. *Notes and Queries on Anthropology*, 1951, p. 192.
10. *Ibid.*, p. 192.
11. Lowie, 1912, p. 41.
12. Boas, 1916, p. 326.
13. Tylor, 1899, p. 143.
14. *Ibid.*, p. 144.
15. *Ibid.*, p. 148.

Chapter 1

1. See Cuoq, 1886, pp. 312-313.
2. *Handbook of North American Indians*, art. "Totemism."
3. Warren, 1885, pp. 43-44.
4. Hilger, 1960, p. 60.
5. Jenness, 1935, p. 54.
6. Firth, 1930-1931, p. 292.
7. Firth, 1930-1931, p. 296. This book was already in proof when there came into our hands a very recent work by Firth (1961) in which other versions of the same myth are to be found.
8. Jakobson and Halle, 1956, Chap. V.
9. Firth, 1930-1931, pp. 300, 301.
10. Firth, 1930-1931, p. 398.
11. Best, 1924.
12. Prytz Johansen, 1954, p. 9.
13. *Ibid.*, p. 85.
14. *Ibid.*, p. 198.

Chapter 2

1. Van Gennep, 1920, p. 351.
2. Elkin, 1933a, p. 66.
3. See above, p. 12.
4. Warner, 1958, p. 117.
5. *Ibid.*, p. 122.
6. *Ibid.*, pp. 122-123.
7. Stanner, 1936.
8. Strehlow, 1947, p. 72.
9. Elkin, 1933b, p. 131.

Chapter 3

1. Malinowski, 1948, p. 27.
2. *Ibid.*, p. 28.
3. *Loc. cit.*
4. Radcliffe-Brown, 1929 [1952, p. 122].
5. *Ibid.*, p. 123.
6. *Ibid.*, p. 129.
7. Malinowski, 1929, Vol. II, p. 499.
8. McConnel, 1930, p. 183.
9. Spencer and Gillen, 1904, pp. 160-161.

10. Firth, 1930-31, p. 297.
11. *Ibid.*, p. 395.
12. Firth, 1939, p. 65.
13. Crosse-Upcott, 1956, p. 98.

14. Radcliffe-Brown, 1939, [1952, pp. 148-149].
15. Kroeber, 1952, p. 306.
16. Durkheim, 1925, p. 332.
17. *Ibid.*, p. 313.

Chapter 4

1. Fortes, 1945, pp. 141-142.
2. *Ibid.*, p. 143.
3. *Ibid.*, p. 144.
4. *Ibid.*, p. 145.
5. Firth, 1930-1931, p. 393.
6. Evans-Pritchard, 1956b, p. 108.
7. Evans-Pritchard, 1956c, p. 80.
8. *Loc. cit.*
9. *Ibid.*, p. 90: "poetic metaphors."
10. *Loc. cit.*

11. *Ibid.*, p. 82.
12. Evans-Pritchard, 1960, p. 19.
13. Evans-Pritchard, 1956c, p. 132.
14. Cf. above, pp. 61-62.
15. Radcliffe-Brown, 1951, p. 113.
16. Cf. above, pp. 12, 61.
17. Radcliffe-Brown, 1951, p. 114.
18. *Ibid.*, p. 116.
19. *Ibid.*, p. 123.
20. *Ibid.*, p. 118.

Chapter 5

1. Bergson, 1958, p. 192.
2. *Loc. cit.*
3. *Ibid.*, pp. 193-194.
4. *Ibid.*, p. 195.
5. *Loc. cit.*
6. Cf. above, p. 73.
7. Durkheim, 1925, p. 318.
8. *Ibid.*, pp. 340-342.

9. *Ibid.*, pp. 284-285.
10. Dorsey, 1894, p. 435.
11. Bergson, 1958, p. 221.
12. Rousseau, 1776, p. 63.
13. *Ibid.*, pp. 41, 42, 54.
14. *Ibid.*, p. 40.
15. Rousseau, 1783, p. 565.

Index